# BUDDHISM

Frank Rainer Scheck
Manfred Görgens

**BARRON'S**

**Cover photos from top to bottom and left to right:**
Buddha-head from Tumshuq, central Asia (SMPK, Museum für Indische Kunst, Berlin) / The
"all-seeing" eyes of the Buddha on the gold-plated square top above the anda of the stupa
of Swayambunath near Kathmandu, Nepal (Photo Günter Heil, Berlin) / Monk of the
Japanese Kegon sect, meditating in the branches of a tree. Japanese scroll, 14th c. (detail) /
Rectangle, triangle, circle. Sepia drawing by Sengai, Idemitsu Museum, Tokyo / Kalachakra
mandala (Photo Martin Brauen, Bern) / His Holiness, the 14th Dalai Lama (Photo dpa) /
Votive stupa from Gandhara (Photo Manfred Görgens, Wuppertal) / Leaf from the Bodhi Tree
of Bodh Gaya, India (Photo Jürgen Bringenberg, Wuppertal) / View of the Magao Caves near
Dunhuang, China (Photo Erhard Pansegrau, Berlin)
**Back cover photos from top to bottom:**
Novice monks at the Golden Stone at the Kyaiktiyo pagoda, Burma (Photo allOver, Josef
Beck) / Buddhist monks as copyists. Painting in the ruins of the monastery near Kara-Shahr,
central Asia (British Museum, London) / Footprints of the Buddha Shakyamuni. Thangka
from Newar, Nepal (Photo Martin Brauen, Bern)
**Background:** Buddha and bodhisattva statues from the Swat Valley, Pakistan
**Frontispiece:** Monk in front of the hand of a colossal Buddha statue. Sukhothai, Thailand
(Photo allOver, Josef Beck)

American text version by: Editorial Office Sulzer-Reichel, Rösrath, Germany
Translated by: Marion Kleinschmidt, Bludenz, Austria
Edited by: Bessie Blum, Cambridge, Mass.

First edition for the United States and Canada
published by Barron's Educational Series, Inc., 1999.

First published in the Federal Republic of Germany in 1999 by
DuMont Buchverlag GmbH und Co. Kommanditgesellschaft, Köln.

Text copyright © 1999 DuMont Buchverlag GmbH und Co. Kommanditgesellschaft,
Köln, Federal Republic of Germany.

Copyright © 1999 U.S. language translation, Barron's Educational Series, Inc.

*All inquiries should be addressed to:*
Barron's Educational Series, Inc.
250 Wireless Boulevard
Hauppauge, New York 11788
http://www.barronseduc.com

*Library of Congress Catalog Card No. 98–72949*

ISBN   0–7641–0910–3

Printed in Italy by Editoriale Lloyd

# Contents

# Preface

Can a "crash course" do justice to a world religion? Is it possible to sum up the spiritual developments of over 2,500 years in a booklet containing not even 200 pages? When the authors were approached by the publisher in regard to this book about Buddhism, these questions arose together with personal memories of the authors' first trips to Asia, memories of how urgently we had sought for a basic text to put into perspective and make sense of a myriad of religious impressions, among them those pertaining to Buddhism.

The lotus, symbol of perfection, grows in all purity out of the mud of samsara. Its stem represents the axis of the world, its leaves sprout out in all directions.

After much consideration, the attempt to clarify the main ideas of one of the world's great religions—a religion that originated with a wise man in north India, whose teachings came to influence large portions of India, south and east Asia, and continue to play an active role today—seems justified. If you are already informed about the fundamental tenets of Buddhism and are looking for a scholarly exposition, this book will not meet your needs. It seeks much more to serve as a basic guide to the subject.

In conclusion, we would like to point out two difficulties, which nevertheless address themselves mainly to scholarly circles. First, it was not always possible to synchronize the illustrations with the corresponding passages of the text. This was partly due to the fact that early Buddhism—according to the evidence of surviving artifacts—was a pictureless time, and in part to the almost hopeless undertaking of adequately illustrating philosophical propositions.

Secondly, a still more daring acrobatic feat was necessary to "translate" foreign concepts, stemming from an unusually large cultural area with distinct systems of writing. Scholars of India and Tibet, sinologists etc. would surely have approved of the use of diacritical signs, but the book would have become incomprehensible for lay readers. We are aware that the terms we have chosen are open to debate, but for the sake of simplicity and clarity, we have used the forms most commonly found in the popular-scholarly works appearing in Asia in Latin script.

Köln/Wuppertal, February 1999, F. R. S./M. G.

"The Buddhist religion expresses the beauty of evening, a perfected sweetness and calm—it represents thankfulness for all that is past; including, what was missing: The bitterness, the disappointment, the rancor; finally: The high, spiritual love; the cleverness of philosophical debate has been left behind, Buddhism is resting from these conflicts, but from these it still derives its spiritual glory, the glow of a setting sun."

*Friedrich Nietzsche,*
The Will to Power

Ashoka pillar. Lumbini, Nepal

The birthplace of the Buddha, a destination for thousands of pilgrimages from around the world, is in Nepal, in a town called Lumbini near the border with India, not far from the foothills of the Himalayan mountains. There, on a polished sandstone pillar, the following words are inscribed: "King Priyadarshi, the favorite of the gods, personally visited and revered this site twenty years after his coronation, where the Enlightened One, the Wise One from the family of the Shakya, was born."

Priyadarshi, known to the world as Emperor Ashoka (ruled ca. 268–239 BC), passed edicts that were instrumental in spreading the teachings of the Buddha, which were initially confined to a small community of monks, over all of India as well as through large areas of Asia. The road to the successful dissemination of these teachings was prepared by a spiritual reform driven by a need for change from what were for many oppressive traditions and inflexible doctrines.

The late Vedic era in Indian history, roughly 900–500 BC, was marked by certain repressive institutions. After the Aryan immigration, the Vedas proclaimed the existence of 33 gods, for whom sacrificial meals had to be prepared on earth. The priests who called on the individual gods to guide them via incantations down to dinner, enjoyed a special social status. Over the course of time, the priestly class, or Brahmans, sought to enhance their standing, and concomitantly, came to abuse their privileged position. Eventually society grew more stratified. In addition to the Brahmans, other castes (*varna*, originally a distinction by color) evolved: these included the warriors (*kshatriya*), who were a caste above tradespeople, artisans, and farmers (*vaishya*), themselves above the ordinary villager (*vish*). But all of the latter were excluded from "knowledge" (*veda*) of cosmic interconnections. The priests guarded their traditions closely and their rituals and poetry were kept secret.

The indigenous peoples subjected by the Aryan invaders were by birth degraded to the rank of servants

"The real impossibility of talking adequately about Buddhism lies in Buddhism itself. When the difficulties seem to lighten, the scope of the dilemma becomes visible. The essence of Buddhism is expressed not in words that describe, but in words that grow silent."

Heinrich Zimmer,
Yoga and Buddhism

Blind Brahman being led by a young ascetic holding a reliquary. Slate relief from Gandhara, north Pakistan, ca. 2nd c. AD

**Buddhism in Southern Asia**

**after mid-3rd millennium BC**
Zenith of Harappa culture in the Indus valley

**after 1500**
Immigration of the Indo-Aryans

**after 1000**
Aryans expand toward the east

**late 6th c.**
Achaemenids conquer northwest Asia; development of empires in India

**477 (?)**
Death of Mahavira, founder of Jainism

**5th c. (?)**
The Buddha lives

**327–325**
Alexander the Great reaches the Indus River

**268**
Emperor Ashoka of the Maurya dynasty usurps the throne of Magadha; first Indian Empire

**ca. 250**
Buddhist council in Pataliputra; Mahinda brings Buddhism to Lanka (Ceylon)

**ca. 183**
Bactrians, originally a Greek people, rule in Gandhara, especially King Menandros supports Buddhism

**1st c.**
Shatavahanas on the Deccan promote Buddhist art; development of Mahayana; in Sri Lanka, the Pali Canon is written down

**ca. 75**
Scyths in Gandhara, followed by the Kushanas, who carry the Buddhist teachings into central Asia

(*shudra*) or expelled as untouchables (*paria*); their fate was inexorable for it was dictated by the Brahmans' spiritual teachings. Where the belief system had once determined that a person's deeds during his or her lifetime would send him either to the gods or to hell upon death, the new belief system held that his or her life merely determined and justified his next existence, or incarnation. Birth (*jati*), life, existence in human, animal, or divine form, terrible suffering or jubilation on earth—nothing was accidental or incidental; and nothing could be averted or altered during any given phase of existence. The sum of what has been accomplished, good and bad deeds combined (*karman*), determined the next form of existence.

Jati, then, became the key to Indian society. Rebirth was ineluctable: Again and again, in an eternal cycle (*samsara*), the previous life demanded its tribute of reward or retribution. It is not difficult to see how the extant political and social structures were sanctioned and solidifed by such a system of belief. Meanwhile,

**78 AD**
Beginning of the Shaka era, which may be identical with the first year in the rule of Kushana king Kanishka (older date)

**1st/2nd c.**
First images of the Buddha

**ca. 150**
Birth of Nagarjuna

**225**
Beginning of the Kanishka era (new date); fall of the Shatavahanas

**249**
Invasion of the Persian Sassanids in Gandhara

**ca. 275**
Vakatakas on the Deccan promote Buddhist art

**320**
Rise of the Gupta dynasty, which extends its influence over all of northern and central India, heyday of Indian art

**4th c.**
In northern India the Yogacara reaches its zenith with the brothers Asanga and Vasubandhu; fading of Buddhism in southern India

**399–414**
Faxian travels in India

**400–500 (?)**
Buddhaghosha, famous Pali teacher in Sri Lanka

**440**
Founding of the Nalanda monastery

**455–500**
Invading hords of White Huns in Gandhara destroy Buddhist monasteries

the spiritual/social system acquired a metaphyiscal dimension revolving around the question of whether it was possible to escape from samsara. Clearly, the cycle of reincarnation is a fundamentally meaningless entanglement unless some means of liberation, some way out, exists: Can *atman*, the "self" at the heart of every being, conquer the desire, the craving for life and rebirth, to become one with *brahman*, the universal spirit?

The answer of the Hindu philosophers was that such liberation lay in recognition that Brahman and atman were fundamentally one and the same: No universal force created, maintained, and destroyed the universe, but merely the self alone. *Tat tvam asi* was the formula that expressed this insight in a nutshell: This is you! But this theory found no simple, general acceptance; it remained the subject of heated, often abstruse, debate from which complex and contradictory conclusions were drawn. These teachings offered no simple message for the masses. Ascetics turned from these debates in disgust, seeking personal liberation in extreme self-mortification, in the effort to become god-like through the almost magical increase of power over the self. But from this approach, too, the masses were excluded.

A new way of thought became an ever more pressing issue as the Aryans moved further eastward,

The Ganges near Varanasi (Benares), north India.

Gomateshvara, one of the mythic precursors of Mahavira. Colossal statue from 983 AD in Shravana Belgola, south India. The "Makers of River Crossings" (*tirthankara*) of Jainism are always depicted naked in contrast to the Buddha.

along the course of the River Ganges. In the face of new cultures and new challenges, the involuted, rigid forms of Brahman thought seemed less and less relevant. As the authority of the brahmans diminished, the military rulers, the kshatriya, increasingly dominated both secular and spiritual matters.

The advance of the Persian king Darius I along the Indus at the end of the 6th century BC brought about a profound transformation. Suddenly a much larger world opened up before the Indian rulers; confronted with a new economic, political, and social system, their own exploits on the Ganges dwindled into relative insignificance. The ensuing trade with the West brought about a flourishing of the East, as new Indian kingdoms and seats of power arose.

As the 6th-century BC world expanded, the rigidity of the old world order was felt as an increasingly painful burden. Spiritual reassessment became inevitable. It was no coincidence that these profound changes occurred not at the periphery of the Indian subcontinent but at its most civilized center: Magadha, one of the new kingdoms in northern India and one of the country's agricultural centers, produced in succession two men who broke with the Vedic traditions, abandoned the belief in a heaven populated by a wide array of deities, and founded religious orders of an entirely new kind that were to attain great influence: Mahavira, the "Great Hero" of ascetic Jainism, and, more especially, the prince Siddhartha Gautama, the Buddha.

**5th/6th c.**
Fall of the Gupta empire; Hindu dynasties on the Deccan
**6th c.**
Development of the Vajrayana
**606–647**
Northern India under King Harshavardhana who promotes Buddhism—along with other religions
**629–645**
Chinese monk Xuanzang travels in India
**637, 710–713**
Arabs invade Sind
**770**
Founding of the Pala dynasty, last promoters of Buddhism in India
**around 800**
Shivaism replaces Buddhism in Kashmir
**998–1030**
Mahmud of Ghazni plunders northern India
**after ca. 1000**
Renaissance of the Theravada in Sri Lanka
**1095**
Palas are replaced by Hindu Senas
**1186–1204**
Muslim Ghorids conquer northern India
**1250**
End of Buddhism in India with the decline of the last Bengal princedom (Pattikhera)
**1505**
Portuguese sailors reach Sri Lanka; enforced conversion to Christianity and economic crash lead to a crisis of the Theravada
**Mid-18th c.**
Buddhism in Sri Lanka revived by monks from Burma and Thailand

**11**

## Dates and legends

At the end of the 19th century, a French scholar argued that the Buddha had no basis in history, but was actually a figure from a sun mythology—a claim that seems astounding to modern ears. Such an academic conclusion is not so surprising considering that, for many years, Buddhist scholarship was confined to such fairy tale-like sources as the *Lalitavistara* ("Development of the Divine Game"), a collection of texts dating over several centuries that clothes the Buddha's life in a web of marvelous reports and erases the Master's historical contours. In addition, according to the original teachings, neither the verification of a historical person nor research into the Buddha's earthly existence is of any significance for the path to enlightenment; worse still, reverence for the Buddha as man leads to disastrous errors.

Shortly after his death, the historical Buddha came to be thought of not as a unique individual, but as a recurring phenomenon that manifests itself again and again, this last time namely as Siddhartha Gautama (in the Pali language: Siddhatta Gotama), the son of a king. Other *tathagatas* (a title for the Buddha that essentially expresses this very idea: It means "thus-gone" or "He who has come and gone as former Buddhas") had appeared long before the historical Buddha. But all had proclaimed the same teaching, the wisdom resulting from innumerable previous existences. Early on, the number of previous tathagatas was placed at seven, the last being Siddhartha, who in turn will be followed by the future savior Maitreya. The use of the word "savior" however, should not lead one to identify Maitreya with the Judeo-Christian conception of the Messiah. In Buddhist teaching, after ages of darkness and ignorance, Maitreya will again take the path of the Buddha, transforming the mere possibility of liberation into an exemplary reality.

The historical Buddha, known as Shakyamuni ("The Sage of the Shakya Clan"), was born into a northern Indian family. Shakya princes were seated in

Maitreya, the future Buddha. Fire-gilded bronze of the 13th c., Nepal.

Buddha in the guise of an elephant enters the body of his mother Maya. Stone relief from Bharhut, north India, 2nd/1st c. BC.

**The legend of the Buddha's birth (according to the *Lalitavistara*)**

The legend of the Buddha's birth begins with an angel looking down with compassion from the Tushita heaven onto the suffering beings on earth, yearning for their deliverance. In another version, the unborn Buddha comes to Maya in the form of a white elephant. Like Mary, the "Mother of God," Maya, the wife of King Shuddhodana, had lived in chastity until this point. In a dream she is carried by a cloud into a heavenly palace where the white elephant, without causing any pain, enters her side. The idea of an "immaculate" conception is thus not unique to Christianity; it may well have originated in ancient India.

After a ten-month pregnancy Maya gave birth in a wondrous manner: A journey led her to the park of Lumbini. There, as Maya stood under a teak tree holding a branch in her right hand, the child emerged from her right hip. Conscious of his earlier existences, the newborn, already in the form of a small child, arose from his bed of lotos blossoms in order to take seven steps and looked toward each of the four corners of the earth. Then the child, who already spoke several languages, proclaimed that he would find liberation (see photo page 14). In fact, all his abilities were marvelous, whether in wrestling or in mathematics, but he most particularly excelled in archery. On the fifth day of his earthly life he was given the name Siddhartha, which means "One who has attained his goal." The name Gautama comes from a Brahman who was an advsisor to the Shakya king. One week after his birth, the Buddha's mother died. Her sister Mahaprajapati took over the child's upbringing and later became Shuddhodana's wife. It was Mahaprajapati who would later convince the Buddha to establish an order for nuns (see page 20).

Maya gives birth to the Buddha from her hip. Slate relief from Gandhara, north Pakistan, 2nd c. AD.

Kapilavastu (probably Tiraulakot in Nepal) and were also in possession of a partially autonomous province in the large kingdom of Koshala. In the park of Lumbini, near the capital, Siddhartha Gautama, the future Buddha, was born the son of the king Shuddhodana and his wife Maya (her name translates literally as "illusion") in about 500 BC. In older literary sources the year of his birth is usually set as 563, but newer theories point to the 5th or even the 4th century BC. Buddhist tradition places the date—surely mistakenly—before 600 BC.

All sources agree, however, on the age of the Buddha at his death: He was eighty years old. At the age of 29, he left his wife, his son, and the house of his parents, attained Awakening (in earlier literature—Enlightenment) six years later, and then dedicated the rest of his life to spreading his teachings. A fragmentary biography can be pieced together out of the teachings that have been handed down, but the legends that sprung up, in particular about his youth as a prince, are far richer and livelier. In the retelling of his biography, of his transformation from prince to ascetic, and thence to his Awakening and teaching, there is really no way to discern what is fact and what is fiction.

### The prince as ascetic
Anyone who is raised in luxury but turns voluntarily to self-mortification in order to follow an uncertain path to awakening is either a desolate outcast or a thoroughgoing visionary. Later Buddhist writings loved to dwell on the unusual transformation from prince to ascetic, making the most of the juxtaposition between the joys and wealth of the parental

The Buddha Shakyamuni as a boy shortly after his birth. The child is standing on a lotos, pointing to heaven and earth. Chinese bronze from the Ming Dynasty (1368–1644), modeled on a Gandharan original.

palace and the deprivations endured in years of extreme castigation.

At his parents' palace, which was probably actually a fairly modest court, the temptations of life were virtually forced upon young Siddhartha. A prophesy had warned his father that his son would either become the universal ruler or the universal teacher: The former, if the sight of earthly misery were kept from him, the latter, if an ascetic clearly showed him how to escape from worldly suffering. Shuddhodana therefore tried to turn his palace into a gilded cage for his son and was overjoyed when Siddhartha fell in love with and married his cousin, the princess Yashodhara. The two soon had a son. But luxury came to feel like a burden to Siddhartha and impelled him to ride out to Kapilavastu three times, and on each of these rides he encountered something that he had never seen before: The first time he came upon an aged man, the second time, a man, terribly ill with the plague, and the third time he saw a dead body in a funeral procession. He had, until then, been completely sheltered from old age, illness, and death.

His dismay at the suffering necessarily attending human life left him no peace, and the prince rode out to the city again. On this fourth ride, a wandering ascetic crossed his path. The wanderer declared that by turning away from everything worldly, he had attained an inner peace beyond joy and suffering. This encounter struck Siddhartha like a revelation: Suddenly he was aware of his mission, of the purpose of his earthly existence.

Secretive, nocturnal exodus of Siddhartha, the prince's son, from his parents' palace. Depiction in a manuscript from 1776, Thonburi, Thailand. The prince is riding the horse Kanthaka, genies (*apsaras*) carry the horse's hooves smothering any sound, while the god Indra closes the horse's mouth to prevent his neighing. The demonic lord Mara (here with four heads) tries to hold back the prince with earthly temptations. Siddhartha's stable hand Chandaka is clinging to the horse's tail.

"Shortly thereafter, I, the black-haired youth, happy in my childhood and newly a man, shaved my head and beard and traded luxurious garments for the yellow cowl against the longings of my father and my mother who protested tearfully. I left my home and moved into homelessness."

*From Buddhas discourse on the right kind of search,* Majjhi-manikaya *26*

The Buddha as ascetic. Modern bronze sculpture modeled on an original from Gandhara. Chiang Mai, Thailand.

Buddha's discourses, as they have been passed down into our times, do not indulge in the vivid, picturesque quality of the legends. In plain language the Master describes his renunciation, his final departure from the palace into homelessness. He left behind everything, even his name. As a wandering exiled monk (*shramana*) Gautama studied for a time the teachings of the Brahmans Arada Kalama and Udraka Ramaputra, but he found in their theories only the very rigidity and inescapable bondage to the temporal he was trying to transcend. Along with five other monks, he decided to turn to meditation and asceticism according to the methods of different influential shramans. In particular, he studied the teachings of Mahavira, who looked on each individual act, even an involuntary or unintentional one, as proof of bondage to the body and therefore as a further entanglement in the net of reincarnations. For him, liberation could only lie in inactivity, which taken to its extreme, meant deliberate starvation.

After years of extreme austerity and self-mortification, Gautama, already near death, realized that neither peace nor virtue was to be found on the path of Mahavira, the founder of Jainism. That way led only to a new, even more tormented confrontation with human transitoriness. As Gautama, much to the distress of his family, had once renounced all luxury, so to the distress of his five companions he ended this stage of his journey to find wisdom and liberation with the most natural act in the world: He ate some rice and took a bath in the river. The end of asceticism marked a further step on his journey away from all previous teachings and the beginning of the great path between joy and suffering.

## Awakening under the Bodhi tree and "setting in motion the wheel of dharma"

According to legend, on the day of Siddhartha's birth, a fig tree (*Ficus religiosa*) had sprouted in the forest of Uruvela, near what is today Gaya in northern India. The Shakya-child now recognized the tree, walked around it thoughtfully, and prepared to remain there until his Awakening.

Remember: The cycle of human suffering, which continues endlessly through continuous reincarnations, demands some kind of release or liberation, but no such liberation was to be found in an acceptable form in any of the traditional teachings. The aim of the Shakyamuni Siddhartha Gautama was both to find a clear irrefutable solution to an intellectual problem and to experience something beyond temporality. His strategy was to attain this not through the ascetic slaughter of the body and its vital functions, but through spiritual contemplation, in seclusion from earthly distractions, and through a conscious or heightened experience of reality, freed from sensual desires. It seems to be true that the person who meditates reaches the most profound level of the Indian spiritual world during night vigils: It is one of the mysteries of the human psyche that, once it has passed the point of complete exhaustion, a kind of euphoria develops that allows him or her to approach old problems and questions in a radically new way.

Let us return to the legend: Gautama spent his night vigils torn between extremes. The personified Earth, already aware of the coming Awakening, stood

Leaf from the Bodhi Tree of Bodh Gaya; the original tree was destroyed by the Bengal king Shashanka (died 625 AD). The giant tree now standing in Bodh Gaya is an offshoot of the 2200 year old tree in Anuradhapura, which in turn is said to stem from the original tree.

Siddhartha, meditating under the Bodhi tree, is beset by the demon Mara. Palm leaf miniature from 1177, north India.

Monks in front of the Dhamekh Stupa made of stones and bricks (4th to 5th c. AD) in Sarnath, north India. Here the Awakened One held his first discourse.

The Buddha's first discourse. Five monks in vestments listen to the insights of the Awakened One. The two gazelles are icons for the Deer Park of Sarnath. Schematically drawn copy of a 13th-c. Burmese mural from Temple 499 in Pagan, Burma.

supportively on one side, whereas the demon Mara, fearing for his power, tried through torments and temptations to divert the meditator from his path to Enlightenment. But neither voluptuous temptresses nor bloodthirsty devils nor the promise of authority over all the world could deter Gautama. In successive night vigils, no longer disturbed even by Mara, Gautama arrived at Enlightenment, or, in mundane terms, at the solution to the problem. The *bodhisattva*, "one awaiting Awakening" became the *Buddha*, the "Awakened."

After seven days and seven nights of contemplation, the Buddha lingered under the fig tree for another four weeks. During this time, Mara tormented the Buddha with a final temptation: Since the Awakening cannot be formulated in words, and the way there cannot be turned into a method, he would have no means of explaining his insights to the people. Instead of trying to assist the ignorant, he should therefore leave his mortal shell and enter *nirvana*—the extinguishing of earthly desire (see page 44). But the Buddha also overcame this temptation, determined to teach the "Middle Path" to his fellow men, the way to peace, wisdom, Awakening, and to the ultimate goal: Nirvana. He came to the Deer Park, near Sarnath, where he encountered his five former companions, who were still pursuing asceticism and at first ridiculed him as a glutton. But then they listened to his discourse of the Four Noble Truths, with which the wheel of teaching, the *Dharmachakra*, was inexorably set in motion.

**Missionary years**

The tranquility of the scene in the Deer Park, where even the animals listened to the words of the Buddha, made up for previous misadventures, for before he had come to the Deer Park, the Awakened One had made an impression on two tradesmen, Trapusa and Bhallika, with his thoughts in Bodh Gaya; but when he wanted to present his teachings to the two Brahman priests whose student he had once been, he unfortunately learned they had already died. He then had an almost ludicrous encounter with a wandering ascetic, who dashed away after hearing only the first few words of the Buddha's discourse. In Sarnath, therefore, the Buddha was more cautious and presented his teachings to the friends who had practiced asceticism with him. The critical turning point came when these strict ascetics found themselves overwhelmed by the profound insights set forth in the discourse and declared themselves ready to assist the Awakened One in his mission.

What followed were 45 years of wandering through the northeastern part of the Indian subcontinent, years in which the numbers of the Buddha's followers grew rapidly. In many places even today one can see larger-than-life "footprints" carved into stones by masons after a visit by the Awakened One. According to legend, a lotos tree sprouted up out of each of the Buddha's steps. The lotos, whose blossoms had been the infant Siddhartha's first bed, embodies both beauty and permanence (see page 7): Its seed, as botanists today may affirm, is still able to germinate after a thousand years. It is a fitting metaphor for the teachings of the Buddha.

In various places in India and southeast Asia, footprints of the Awakened One hewn into stone are on display. In Bodh Gaya, north India, these footprints are copied onto cotton and sold to pilgrims as pious souvenirs.

At first the Buddha concentrated on teaching the educated elite of the warrior caste (*kshatriya*). He sometimes also converted Brahman priests, but his encounters with the masses tended to be limited to comforting words; their simple religious beliefs allowed no easy inroads into the new complex teachings. There were rumors of spectacular events taking place at the royal courts, and these rumors contributed to the

popularization of the Buddha's teachings. King Bimbisara of Magadha and many of his subjects became his lay disciples, and Prasenajit of Koshala enjoined the Buddha to enter a competition with selected thinkers from other schools.

Verbal dueling, in which the winners received great prizes, had a long tradition. One highly celebrated Brahman named Yajnavalkya used elaborate ruses to impress his listeners and earn himself material rewards, but the Buddha sought debate only in order to convince his fellow men of the truth. Legend tells that strange wonders attended the debate, a sign of the power emanating from the righteousness of the Awakened One.

The fact that the Buddha undertook missionary work is already proof of the humaneness of his teachings, which attempted to address the troubles of mankind. Instead of caste, intellect and a spirit of openness became decisive in finding the way to liberation. Thus, the Indian subjection to fate could be discarded, and the reward for improving one's life was no longer fundamentally bound to a later incarnation.

The Buddha took his last revolutionary step after returning to his parents' home after 32 years, where he led his family to the Middle Path (see page 18). Prompted by conversations with his adopted mother Mahaprajapati, the Buddha finally agreed that women be given the opportunity to follow the path of liberation and that an order for nuns should be founded. Here, equality between men and women was established in a way that remained impossible for most of the world's great religions for centuries—or millennia—to come.

At the age of 80, while the Buddha was staying in Kushinagara (today Kashia, Bihar), he ate a meal which sources call "sukara-maddava," a special pork dish. However, since Buddhists are not allowed to kill, it seems unlikely that he in fact ate a meal of meat.

The Buddha of the Great Miracle of Shravasti, known also as the Fire and Water Miracle. The Buddha proves himself lord over the elements, as flames lash out of his shoulders and water streams from his feet. Sculpture from Afghanistan, ca. 3rd c. AD. Shravasti, today Maheth on the border to Nepal, was in the Buddha's day capital of the Koshala Kingdom. Supposedly the Awakened One was active in the nearby Jetavana monastery for 25 years and worked many wonders there.

Buddhist "nuns" in Burma. These are so-called Eight Commandment Women, whose status is not identical to that of ordained monks—they have further rules to obey. In Hinayana countries, Buddhist orders for women or women cloisters no longer exist.

Perhaps it was a mushroom. In any case, the historical Buddha died of food poisoning. He passed out of the world but left behind the light of his teaching.

As was the custom, the citizens of Kushinagara cremated the mortal remains. But, according to legend, the city became the victim of a siege for so doing. Eight different rulers vied to take possession of the ashes, until finally a Brahman advised them to divide the remains among themselves. They did so, and on taking them to their separate kingdoms, had the ashes buried under eight burial mounds.

The conflict over the Buddha's ashes is settled through the mediation of the Brahman Drona (represented in the middle): The ashes are divided among the eight rulers of north India. Originally columns flanked the scene left and right. Slate relief from Gandhara, north Pakistan, 3rd c. AD.

### First monastic order

The first to enter the new order or community (*sangha*) of "mendicant monks" (*bhikshu*) were Trapusa and Bhallika, in addition to the Buddha's five former monk companions already mentioned: Ashvajit, Bhadrajit, Kaundinya, Mahanama, and Vaspa. Then, the son of a merchant from Varanasi (Benares), Yasha, who suffered from depressions, managed through the Buddha's aid to conquer his mental illness and joined the group; 54 young men

from this city on the Ganges followed his example. After being guided into the new teachings, or *dharma*, they separated again, each taking his own way through the country, living on the alms contributed by lay believers. The latter were especially numerous in the growing class of tradespeople. Their compassion and good deeds would be rewarded, in spiritual terms, in rebirth at a level nearer to the Awakening. No one, moreover, who wished to commit himself (or herself, as mentioned above) to the rules of the order was turned away.

One of the "Eldest" (*sthavira*) who spread the Buddhist doctrine in the first mission. Tibetan painting from the 18th or 19th c.

Lay believers were required to obey five injunctions that in no way conflicted with their daily lives in the world: They were not to kill any living thing; they were to take nothing that was not given to them freely; they were not to do wrong because of sensual desires; they were not to lie, and they were not to consume any intoxicating drinks.

In addition to the five rules for laypeople, monks were required also to fast after the midday meal, not to indulge in entertainments such as music and dancing, not to wear jewelry or cosmetics, not to live in comfortable lodgings, and not to possess money. In later years an extensive catalogue of rules of behavior was formulated and read to the monks at each full and new moon, so that the monks would have the opportunity to confess publicly to any violations. Murder and theft could not be forgiven, nor could the consciously false assertion of having attained Awakening. Sexual contact, considered the strongest bond to the transitory, was also a compelling reason for expulsion from the monastic order.

Monk during his morning begging round on Sri Lanka. Buddhist monks cover their living expenses through alms. The donors, lay believers, are grateful to the monks, as they earn spiritual merits through their gifts.

The Buddha's powers of teaching and persuasion were so great that, even during his lifetime, thousands of people decided to follow the monastic rules. Some contemporaries labeled this movement as a kind of mass escapism, but today most students and scholars of Buddhism seem to agree that the rapid increase in the number of his followers was largely owing to the spiritual charisma of Siddhartha Gautama.

Thai monks at the last meal of the day, taken around noon.

After the Buddha had gained his first followers in Sarnath, he made his way back to Uruvela alone. There he met up with a group of Brahmans, all prominent scholars. The three Kashyapa brothers were the spiritual leaders of this group; one of them, Maha Kashyapa ("The Great Kashyapa") would become head of the First Council and play an important role in the early history of Buddhism. The conversion of these famous, highly respected brothers led hundreds of Brahmans to profess their belief in the Buddha's teachings. These conversions created such a stir that even the attention of King Bimbisara of Magadha was aroused, and he too soon declared himself a lay believer. In this way, a wide cross section of the population became familiar with the new teachings. Two of the Buddha's favorite students were Brahmans from Magadha: Shariputra, famous for his great learning and wisdom, who took over the important function of intermediary to the people, and Maudgalyayana, who was thought to have supernatural powers—these were probably abilities that he had acquired as an ascetic and had developed further through the meditational teachings of the Buddha. Both Shariputra and Maudgalyayana predeceased the Buddha himself.

In his later years, two of his family members accompanied the

Shariputra, one of the Buddha's favorite pupils. Tibetan wooden sculpture with gold plating.

Master on his path of liberation and were in his confidence: His son Rahula and his cousin Ananda. In the canonized writings, the Buddha's speeches often begin with "Thus have I heard." The witness recording his words was Ananda, who was said to have memorized some 84,000 of the Buddha's sayings. It was also

The Brahman Maha Kashyapa. Slate relief from Gandhara, north Pakistan, ca. 2nd c. AD.

Ananda who wept while attending the dying Buddha—quite a natural reaction for most of us but alien to Buddhist monks, as the teachings maintain that earthly existence is suffering and that the departure of the Awakened One is the sign of his liberation.

In contrast to the kind-hearted Ananda, Devadatta, another cousin to Gautama, became infamous.

Devadatta was a strict ascetic who demanded sterner discipline and greater isolation from the world for the community of monks. The result was a confrontation that nearly endangered the missionary work and the future of the monastic order. The threat created by Devadatta developed via legend into a far more dramatic scenario: Ajatashatru, son of King Bimbisara, was preparing to dethrone his father and allied himself with Devadatta against the Buddha, his father's friend and advisor. Attempts were made on Gautama's life, but the supernatural abilities of the Awakened One doomed such efforts to fail. Devadatta evolved into more than the temporal adversary of the historical Buddha; in the tales of Siddhartha Gautama's earlier existences in different guises he appears as the embodiment of evil.

Ananda, as a sign of his conversion, brings the Buddha food. Slate relief from Gandhara, north Pakistan, ca. 2nd c. AD.

### First councils

Although all of the Buddha's discourses are available today in written form and have been translated into every major language, the authenticity of the texts remains open to question. In Vedic times sacred words were traditionally transmitted orally—they were the secret knowledge of the Brahmans, the sacrificial and magical sayings or formulas entrusted to only a few select disciples. Oral transmission remained the primary means of conveying knowledge for centuries following the Shramana Gautama. There is, therefore, no original written canon. The precarious nature of the source material inevitably generates endless speculation about the ultimately unanswerable question regarding original formulations and thoughts. To what degree have voluntary or involuntary modifications introduced by later interpetations, interpolations, opinions, or mere ambiguities of translation altered the Buddha's teachings? Translating the words of the Awakened One into Western languages poses particular difficulties owing to entirely different verbal and conceptual associations.

The historical Buddha as teacher and advisor met with people from all kinds of backgrounds. He took on their worries even to the point of considering their material welfare, and he always regarded individual circumstances as the basis or framework for decisions. This tolerance, paradoxically enough—

Illuminated Buddhist palm leaf text dating from 1156 from Bihar, north India (compare also illustration on pages 74/75).

to use a term from Western philosophy—makes concrete articulation of his teachings still more difficult. The term "paradox" is unknown to Indian philosophy; as a phenomenon, it does not refer to a conflict. In contemporary Japanese Zen Buddhism, it is even considered to have great potential to illuminate or clarify (see page 146).

Saptaparni cave in Rajgir, north India. Here the first Buddhist council was supposedly held.

Soon after the Buddha's death, the monastic order had to decide which of the myriad of interpretations and memories of the words of the Awakened One should be collected into a unified canon. In order to establish guidelines, according to legend, 500 of Gautama's most prominent followers assembled in Rajagriha (today, Rajgir), the capital of Magadha, for a council that lasted seven months. The Buddha's cousin Ananda (see page 24) was considered the one best informed, his opinion was consulted, and his decisions accepted in cases of doubt.

On the other hand, this First Council could not forestall further differences of opinion. The Buddha himself had not intended or stipulated a hierarchic order for his followers, recommending only the teachings themselves as a spiritual guide.

About 380 BC, a Second Council supposedly convened in Vaishali, in order to mediate an explosive conflict between the "Way of the Elders" and the "Members of the Great Community" (*mahasanghika*) over the monastic rules. The former, who wished to adhere to the Buddha's unchanged word, emerged victorious, whereas the latter, who accepted later interpretations and commentaries as more meaningful and more relevant to contemporary life, split off. A schism ensued.

Under the Emperor Ashoka (see page 8; page 49) a Third Council convened in Pataliputra (today, Patna)

Text from the Ashoka pillar from Topra, north India, written in Devanagari script. The pillar was brought to Delhi in the 14th c. by Sultan Firoz Shah and still stands there today in the citadel of Kotla, well preserved, its inscription almost complete.

in around 250 BC. Its main goal was to draft statutes for monks. The two main branches of Buddhism, however, could no longer reach consensus; the Mahasanghikas refused to endorse the resolutions of the council. Some hundreds of years later, they convened in Jalandhara (East Punjab), or, according to another tradition, in Kundalavana (Kashmir) and resolved their own written canon—the Mahayana (see page 68).

Worship of the Three Jewels (*triratna*) representing the Buddha, his teachings and the monastic order founded by him. The Buddhist believer daily seeks his refuge in these three jewels. Slate relief from Gandhara, north Pakistan, 2nd c. AD.

## The "Three Jewels" of Buddhism

One becomes a Buddhist neither by birth nor by a formulaic declaration of faith. Anyone who reads the following chapters and perceives the truth of the teachings, in whichever particular form, may consider himself or herself a Buddhist. He or she need follow no rituals or ceremonies, attend no temple, pray to no gods or even to the Buddha. This is not to say that there are no rituals in use throughout all Buddhist countries today; there are. But these are, without exception, later additions. The Buddha himself regarded them at best as useless, but often in fact as an obstacle on the path to knowledge of the Four Noble Truths. Commandments uttered by the Buddha can in no way be equated with the Judeo-Christian Commandments. If ignored, you do not bring down the retributive anger of God against your own person: Such breaches merely signify that the teachings are not yet understood or that the way is still too difficult for the novice. In this light, the moral directives the Buddha taught to lay disciples are a kind of measure of their personal insight, not the mandatory duty of the student of the Christian catechism.

Triratna symbol, surrounded by a flaming mandorla, in a modern Tibetan block print depiction.

The "Three Jewels" (*triratna*) appears as a ritual and sounds like a declaration of faith but is in fact meant to remind the believer of his or her spiritual foundations. It should be spoken three times a day: "I take refuge in the Buddha. I take refuge in the dharma. I take refuge in the sangha."

The Buddha, the first jewel, is neither a prophet nor a god, nor an incarnation of a divine force. He is, rather, an exemplary human being, who, because of his perfection, was able to teach himself and achieve liberation through his own efforts. For his contemporaries, he was a kind of signpost, pointing out the path on which freedom lay. To seek refuge in the Buddha does not signify abject worship, but seeking and valuing the advice of the Awakened One.

After the Master's death, his teachings, based on the insights he gained (*dharma*), became definitive. But this, the second jewel, also requires no unconditional faith. The dharma analyzes our world and human existence, revealing a profound ethical commitment and pointing out a path that will educate and discipline the spirit.

Those who wish to live their lives completely according to the dharma must renounce the world. Economic and social necessities as well as professional and familial ties necessarily lead to conflicts with the teachings and are impediments on the path to liberation. Such individuals enter the monastic orders, or sangha, the third jewel. They are not "priests" as such; rather, they serve as models for lay believers, as mediators to a higher world.

"And the Buddha considered: My locks of hair are not suitable to a monk; but there is no one who is able to shear the hair of a future Buddha. So I will sever it myself with my sword."
*From the Pali canon*

The hair of a Burmese novice being shorn.

Buddhist funeral procession near Kandy, Sri Lanka.

"An Indian doctor, called to see a sick person, will ask him of herself four questions about what might be real in this case. He recognizes four truths. The same is true of the Buddha. First, the doctor will confirm the sickness as real, secondly its real symptoms and roots. From these findings results the third truth, whether the sickness can be cured. Here, the fate of the patient is decided. Uncurable

## Life as suffering

"What, o monks, is the holy truth of suffering? Birth is suffering; aging is suffering; sickness is suffering; death is suffering; sorrow, lamentation, pain, grief, and despair are suffering; association with what one dislikes is suffering; separation from what one likes is suffering; in short, the five existential factors (which make up a person) are suffering."

This was the first of the Four Noble Truths that the Buddha expounded in his first sermon at Sarnath; in it, clearly, life is inevitably linked with suffering. But in both the West and the more sanguine cultures of Southeast Asia, the equation of life and suffering has repeatedly elicited disbelief and consequently been met with rejection. How can something that is experienced as joy be suffering? Bounty, health, friendship—where is the torment here?

Buddhism's answer to this conundrum lies in two apparent truisms. One addresses the finite nature of the individual within time, which is eternal. No accumulation of goods, no doctor, no priest can alter the temporal nature of our individual lives one iota. The only cure is to close one's eyes against the fact of death. Luxury, medicine and religion serve only to comfort and to delude. The second fundamental realization addresses the insubstantiality of everything that exists. A house, for example, is in fact no more than an idea that has taken on a material form: If the house is broken down into its various parts, and these parts are in turn broken down into different building substances, and these are reduced to their organic components, the result is only a material void that can be discerned by neither the mind nor the senses. At the same time, throughout an incomprehensible endlessness, this material void coalesces into the myriad forms of the phenomena that occupy the macrocosm.

Although, for the unhappy person, suffering is obvious, for the apparently happy person, suffering lies in the discovery that joy will not last forever. The story of Gautama's life demonstrates that the recognition of fundamental suffering and the transitory nature of life already spoiled his pleasure in luxury during his youth, and the ascetic life managed only to reconfirm the fact of mortality. In later years, he was conscious of some rare moments of peace that he had experienced under a tree, moments in which his spirit seemed free from the pain and threat of mortality because of the presence of nature. His later Awakening under the bodhi tree was to become the most intense, most profound experience of what he had sometimes felt as a youth.

The list of physical and spiritual sufferings in the sermon of Sarnath encompass the indirect and direct experience of pain, the fear of loss as well as loss itself. "You cannot say of that which is suffering and finite: That is I, that belongs to me, that is my Self." The Buddha's assertion contradicts both the Christian idea of the soul and the theory of the Brahman, according to which the individual has something immutable within him- or herself, and it is this that is reborn.

Nevertheless, the Buddha did not fundamentally reject the cyclical view or the cosmic laws of nature and morality, which, when obeyed or disobeyed, determine the form of rebirth. But the Buddha's idea of nonsubstantiality, the *anatman*, represented a new

diseases are not touched by the Indian (as well as the ancient Greek or Roman) physician. The fourth truth points the way to a cure.
*Heinrich Zimmer,*
Yoga and
Buddhism

The Buddha under the bodhi tree. Contemporary popular depiction from Thailand.

interpretation of these cycles in the eternity and insubstantiality of matter. A fortuitous and timely example is the virtual worlds of the computer, based on nothing more than the flow of energy. If computers were programmed for human deeds and a personal I, they would become a world whose reality could no longer be tested because such a confessional program of personal faith may also be an expression of an inner truth.

According to Buddhist teachings, fateful or evil powers are "five groups of existential factors that cause men to cling to the world" (see marginal text page 34). They are chimeras, phantasms of impersonal forces with no power to exist on their own. The ignorant allow themselves to be deceived, but, on closer scrutiny, these forces reveal themselves as "temporal and full of suffering." When these factors of existence come to interact, they produce in each person the individual subjective experience and the feeling that the I is identical with these temporal processes: But this experience is based on an illusion that will prove to be painful.

The Buddhist truth of suffering, hence, is reinforced in that existence itself is not only transient and full of pain but also without substance. But this is exactly where the possibility of redemption arises. If the nature of existence were in fact permanent and immutable, there could be no hope for escape from its limitations, either mentally nor physically. It is significant that the Buddha neither sought nor wished for awakening regarding the eternity or temporality of time and space. The highest suffering, according to the Buddha, consists not in the human inability to answer cosmic riddles but in unrequited desire—not to attain what is internally most desired, the end of the cycle of rebirths. This great, secret, goal can be achieved through neither desire nor prayer nor metaphysical postulates; instead, first and foremost, one must recognize the causes of suffering.

A boy presents the Buddha with dust—symbol for the transience of the world. Slate relief from the Afghanistan Gandhara tradition, ca. 3rd c. AD.

## Thirst for life as a cause of suffering

"This, o monks, is the sacred truth of the origin of suffering: It is this desire, giving rise to rebirth, accompanied by delight and attachment, finding delight now here now there; namely, sensual desire, desire for eternal existence, the desire for self destruction."

Novices under the bodhi tree in Bodh Gaya, north India.

The temptation is overpowering. The ignorant person, who does not recognize the suffering behind joy, succumbs to desire. Such persons demand sensual pleasures that seem desirable but find in them only confirmation of a self heading toward death, the end of all pleasures. Thirst for life is hence at the root of suffering, the realization and endurance of mortal insufficiency. The body itself provides incontrovertible proof of impermanence, for what does the octogenarian still have left of childhood? Neither one's thoughts, one's sense of self, one's memories, nor even the cells that make up the body have remained the same. How can humans then let themselves be so fundamentally fooled by the world and by desires as to believe in a self that in fact only appears to be real in the present, in a fleeting moment? But, even when the truth of these considerations is recognized, temptations arising from pleasures again beset

Two old Tibetan monks in the Drepung monastery, Tibet.

people, and human life continues to be subsumed in the eternity of suffering.

*Paticcasamuppada* is the Buddhist term for the vicious cycle of "dependent origination." With each step we sink deeper into the quagmire of the suffering that is existence. At the beginning of the chain is ignorance (*aviyya*), resulting in driving forces or predispositions (*sankhara*) seeking to form new existences. These cause consciousness (*vinnana*), which demands "mind" and "form" (*nama-rupa*), out of which the six senses again arise (*salayatana*—five senses and thinking) as the foundation for mental processes. At this point in "dependent origination," conscious impression (*phassa*) becomes possible, which leads to emotion (*vedana*), which in turn calls forth desire (*tanha*). On top of the desire for life (*upadana*), becoming and rebecoming (*bhava*) develop in ways predetermined by desire. This leads to birth (*jati*) and, with it, old age and death (*jara-marana*).

This interconnected causal chain that is so central to Buddhist teachings (here presented in its most common version—several variations exist) came as a revelation to Eastern thinkers. As for the West, Helmuth von Glasenapp and others note that Western thinking usually inverts this chain of causality: Aging and death must be preceded by (re-)birth, and this by the process of becoming, and this again by the proclivity for life. Proclivity for life arises from desire, awakened by feeling. Feelings and responses arise from contact with the external world, which is, however, only experienced through the senses. Only an individual being that already has a consciousness can allow the senses free reign. Consciousness, again, can only result from the physical desires of a previous existence. The physical desires finally lead back to the beginning: The illusion (ignorance), blocking the insight that all of existence is temporal, full of suffering, and insubstantial.

Moreover, the craving for life gives rise to other roots of evil, such as hate and blindness; strife, war,

The early teachings saw five groups of desire for life: *Rupa* (parts of the body, with four elements: The firm = e. g. hair, flesh; the liquid = for example saliva, urine; the hot = e. g. warmth, digestion; wind = e. g. breath, flatulence; these elements are present in any being. They are acquired by karman and do not belong to the being, but nonetheless make up the body); *vedana* (feelings); *sanna* (perceptions and the differentiation between them); *sankhara* (emotional formations and inclinations = the will resulting from the mentioned perceptions); *vinnana* (consciousness, gaining consciousness without content).

murder, and theft signify a malevolent karman that even during the present existence produces obvious suffering. In any case, a life filled with evil words, deeds, and thoughts leads to an increase of suffering in the next world, to a worse rebirth. The individual who tries to find a meaning in these processes only confirms his or her own ignorance of the true nature of the world and serves to distance him- or herself even further from the only true goal, an existence free from greed, hate, or delusion, one with a good karman.

The origin of suffering, thus, comes from within humans themselves, but it is also from within that the causes can be extinguished—in fact, only from within. No other religion places so much emphasis on the individual's power for personal change as does the teaching of the Buddha.

### Extinction of the thirst for life in order to end suffering

"This, o monks, is the holy truth of the cessation of suffering: The utter cessation, without attachment, of that very craving, its renunciation, surrender, release, lack of pleasure in it."

Again and again we lose sight of the important recognition, repeatedly we fall into the position of the doubting, doubtful self, desiring and fighting for what we desire, without considering the price we must pay for what we think is satisfaction. It is the belief in the reality of the self and of our very existence that seems to confer meaning on this desire. In fact, though, it is not even necessary to look at life in terms of the cycle of rebirths to see that suffering necessarily grows out of desire: The

Detail (center of hub) of a Tibetan Wheel of Life (see page 118) depicting aspects of dependent origination (*paticcasamuppada*): The figures on the right are pulled into the nether regions after leading bad lives, whereas the figures on the left are ascending towards nirvana. The three animals at the center of the hub represent the "unsalutary roots" of human blindness: Greed (cock), hate (serpent), and blindness (pig).

Modern monk life on Sri Lanka.

Buddha's ideas about the consumption of meat: People should intend to get by without eating any meat. Monks, considering the rule not to kill, should completely refrain from eating meat. If they are invited for a meal, however, they should only turn down the meat if they are certain that their host slaughtered the animal for their sake only. Otherwise, the rejection would be considered rude toward the host—a graver offence than eating meat.

striving for material goods creates pain for the loser, affection for a new partner causes pain to the one left behind, a ruler causes pain to the ruled, and the feeling of possessing nothing, feelings of loneliness and of subjugation bring about a state of readiness for pain. Brooding over metaphysical questions or searching for a greater meaning in this obvious state of suffering is simply a maneuver to distract us from the essential, that is, from the path toward its dissolution. "He who asks, already errs; who answers, errs equally." However, he or she who tests the chain of causes for the only link open to influence arrives at the same time at the root of evil: At desire that must be dissolved.

Recognition that everything is temporal, full of suffering, and impersonal, illuminates the true nature of desire, stripping it of the illusion that it bears deep meaning. Since life is a necessary corollary of suffering, the hunger for life must be conquered, specifically on the Middle Path between sensual pleasure and asceticism. On this path, the karma-creating factors—greed, hatred, and delusion—disappear. Once these are conquered, the senses are no longer deluded by form, and even such moral supports as the monastic order become superfluous: The need to be distracted from desire no longer exists. Now it is possible to nurture the knowledge that in fact all desire merely blocked the entry to pure joy. This is an important point for those to whom the Buddha's teaching seems inimical to life, for how can one thoroughly enjoy something—possessions, love, existence, whatever—if one blindly goes through life afraid of losing it?

### The Eightfold Path:
### Through self-disciplne to the abolition of suffering

"This, o monks, is the sacred truth concerning the path to the abolition of suffering: This is the sacred Eightfold Path, consisting of right understanding, right thought, right speech, right action, right livelihood, right effort, right mindfulness, right concentration in the self."

Eight steps lead to the dissolution of the desire for life. According to contemporary opinions, these steps should not be accomplished in the order originally described by the Buddha: They should be divided into groups of ascending steps, with the higher steps encompassing the goals of the lower ones.

One must start with a fundamental recognition or insight in order to carry out right speech, action, and livelihood successfully. When these have been per-fected, understanding has also grown. Thus, one may pass from the ethical elements to the elements of inner composure, to effort, mindfulness, and concentration. These, in turn, are prerequisites for the elements of knowledge, that is, for the right thought or cast of mind, and—the

Tibetan novice opening the temple gate.

highest gain—for the perfection of right under-standing. Each of the steps has two levels: One points the way for lay believers, in such actions as giving alms to attain merit in this world (see photo page 23), while the second is directed toward monks.

For lay believers, right understanding signifies the elementary insight that it is necessary to distinguish, in terms of karma, between what is malevolent and what beneficial. Evil acts, acts that are not productive in terms of personal liberation are: The killing of living things, appropriation of others' property, forbidden sexual relations, lying, maligning others, crude language, empty talk, greed, malice, and wishing harm to others. In all of these reside the fundamental evils—desire, hatred, and blindness—the causes of suffering. Renunciation of the malevolent is therefore beneficial for the karma.

Lay believer, probably a noble patron. Relief from the eastern gate of Stupa I in Sanchi, north India, 1st c. BC.

Understanding on a higher plain, on the level of the monk, means understanding the Four Noble Virtues enumerated by the Buddha in the sermon of Sarnath. To embark on this second step, one begins with the Buddha's rejection of useless questions and his focus on gaining insight into the truths. It is by these means that the first fetters that subjugate the spirit are removed: These include love of rituals (in more general terms, holding onto habits), scepticism, and egomania. The latter can take the form of delusions about eternity (e. g., that the self survives death) or about self-annihilation (e.g., that the self is destroyed after death). An increase in knowledge is accompanied by a diminution of sensual desires and of anger, both of which further restrain the spirit. Finally, the fetters that bind one to life itself must be renounced—specifically, the desire for refined, spiritual existence, as well as arrogance, excitation, and ignorance. Such profound liberation, however, can only be attained by the *arhat*, or worthy one, on the highest step of wisdom, awaiting the Awakening. Others may attain the level of *sakadagamin* ("entering the stream") which is followed by only a few more rebirths, or by just one return to the world, or by *anagamin*, which means "he who will never return" to this world, suggesting rebirth into the world of the gods.

Right thought means that all worldly or other-worldly desires are set aside, goodness is the principle of action, and that harm to other living things is avoided. A monk, a rigorous Buddhist, can only consciously form his character to this end through strict training. But once he attains right thought, no incentive can move him to greed, hatred, or violence.

Right speech, perhaps the least strenuous of the steps, initially means rejecting all forms of lying, even those connected with some kind of necessity or politeness. In addition, it is unacceptable to retell information that results in division or discord (as in gossip). The goal of right speech, rather, is mutual understanding and joy in communal harmony. Swearing and small talk are both to be avoided. All speech should be polite, memorable, measured, well founded, and meaningful—only then does it serve higher goals on the Eightfold Path. For the same reason, casual and useless conversations about rulers, warriors, and heroes should be avoided.

Right action lies in not bringing death to other living things, taking nothing that is not given freely, and refraining from unlawful sexual contact. Because of the last injunction, Western critics have often accused Buddhism of a kind of hostility toward the senses. Monks do, in fact, live in complete chastity; lay believers, on the other hand, are only required to avoid sexual contact with young or dependent partners. In the teachings, "dependent" means married or engaged, and includes prisoners or relatives' wards.

Right livelihood pertains to earning a living in a manner that is salutary to the karma, one that does not harm others. The teachings disapprove of trade in living things, in weapons, meat, intoxicating drinks, and poisons. No professions should be chosen in which violence to men or animals is practiced. The same goes for fraud, uncontrolled greed for profit, and attempts to persuade unwilling business partners (extortion). His position toward the enjoyment of intoxicating drugs again demonstrates the sound judgment and insight into human weakness with which the Buddha formulated his rules; he refrains always from pointing the moral

"The monk goes into the forest, sitting at the foot of a tree or in an empty hut. He sits down cross-legged, his body erect, and he directs his attention in front of him. He attentively inhales, he attentively exhales. When he inhales slowly, he knows, 'I inhale slowly;' when he exhales slowly, he knows, 'I exhale slowly.' When he inhales fast, he knows, 'I inhale fast;' when he exhales fast, he knows, 'I exhale fast.' 'With a clear perception of the whole body I want to inhale and to exhale,' thus he trains himself. 'Appeasing this bodily function, I want to inhale and to exhale,' thus he trains himself."

*Mahasati-patthanasutta,*
*D 22*

Tibetan lay believer with prayer wheel. In late forms of Buddhism rituals often replace the original striving for spiritual perfection.

finger and focuses instead on the social consequences of such behavior: The conflict that arises from drunkenness, the loss of health, pecuniary difficulties, and so on.

Right effort involves ridding oneself of bad character traits and increasing the good ones, suppressing evil thoughts and awakening noble ones.

Right mindfulness offers even the non-Buddhist many possibilities to attain peace, sound judgment, and endurance. For Buddhists, the actual goal is to overcome greed, pain, and melancholy, to be fully aware of the moment, to experience with complete clarity the becoming and declining of the body, to find the way to the Middle Path through Buddhist insight and purification.

The exercises of right mindfulness always begin with conscious breathing—in and out with complete attentiveness (see marginal text page 39). Passing thoughts are neither chased away nor suppressed. With increasing practice, distractions will not even occur, and one will be able to concentrate fully on breathing. Eventually, walking, standing, sitting, lying, speaking, eating, drinking, and other actions

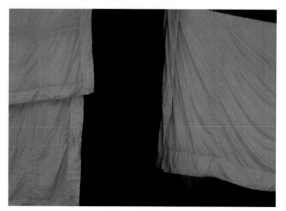

Monks robes hung up to dry in Chiang Mai, Thailand. Robes are traditionally dyed with natural colors by the monks themselves.

Meditating monk in Bodh Gaya, north India.

may be done with equal attentiveness. Concentration on the breath is followed by contemplation of the individual parts of the body. Then, in ascending order, one contemplates, from without, as it were, feelings, the personal state of consciousness, and the so-called objects of the spirit (for example, sensual greed, ill will, excitation, addiction to doubt, corporality). At the end of this highly intricate and complex path, one vanquishes fear, desire, and lassitude. One also enhances one's ability to endure heat, cold, thirst, hunger, and physical and spiritual injury and acquires certain supernatural powers; the latter may become manifest in an ability to see through other beings or to recollect earlier stages of existence.

Right concentration induces a temporary withdrawal from the world whereby all the powers of the spirit are concentrated on a single object, for example, on a lotos blossom. Here, the preceding step becomes more profound; it becomes a kind of waning of consciousness, such as the Buddha himself experienced under the Bodhi tree. The meditative profundity, however, is fleeting, temporally limited, presaging the ultimate insight. A final review of the Four Noble Truths and the Eightfold Path is necessary for the aspirant (*bodhisattva*) to attain permanent Buddhahood and to bring the cycle of reincarnations to an end.

"And in me arose the insight and inner contemplation: The freeing of the spirit is for me immutable. This is the last birth, there is no re-being."

Picture depicting the "Great Daruma" painted by the Zen master Hakuin Ekaku (1685–1768): Viewing one's own nature and becoming a Buddha. The "Daruma" depicted here has cut off his eyelids so as not to fall asleep during meditation.

In the West, asceticism, yoga, and Buddhist meditation are often poorly differentiated and further blurred through the popularization of clichés. Because many people in India and eastern Asia seem to have attained a high degree of control over their bodies, Westerners tend to hold unreasonably high expectations for meditation techniques; the *yogi* (practitioner of yoga) and the Buddhist monk, on the other hand, tie their sense of well-being to a completely different world view and way of life.

For the Buddha, asceticism was a long and—as he himself described it—very painful journey. He practiced the suppression and control of vital bodily functions until he achieved extraordinary "magical powers" that astounded his contemporaries.

The yogi has a different goal, although he also practices asceticism. He concentrates on the training itself: Through the "yoking on" (*yoga*) of mental and physical powers, these very energies are developed to a level they cannot reach in a normal life. These practices go back many thousands of years, probably to the Indus civilization. In non-Buddhist yoga, breathing control remains central. Through arduous exercises, breath, or *prana*, is retarded and no longer is an involuntary function. Great value is placed on holding one's breath. According to the Indian way of thought, prana is synonymous with the essence of existence; it is a sign and cause of not being dead. The goal of breath control is to distill the spirit (or invisible) body out of the visible body.

From his experience with yoga and asceticism, Siddhartha Gautama developed a new and surprisingly effective concept—one that strives for contentment with the moment. All concentration is focused on the perception of what is, on the fully conscious, impartial observation of breathing. The concept of mindfulness is based on the fact that a person who perceives the fundamental experiences of life only in part or falsely will discover that his or her life rests on weak pillars. These inadequate perceptions will inevitably generate further mistaken interpretations. The individual will not understand the quality of his or her existence and will not see his or her own self as the microcosm that breathes, partaking for a short span of time in the macrocosm.

Neither the way of the yogi nor that of the Buddha ends on the level of breathing; both use this discipline (in yoga) or this perception (in Buddhism) to advance to further spiritual levels. In his teachings, the Buddha described four stages of mental deepening, the last of which signified the highest level of tranquility beyond suffering and joy.

**Basic rule**: The novice gives up all worldly occupations for the duration of the session and acknowledges the five rules for lay believers, perhaps even the eight ethical rules for monks. He (or she) must seek refuge in the "Three Jewels" of Buddhism, cultivate kind thoughts in regard to all beings, put aside pleasure in his own body, and recognize the imminence of his own death. The following exercises are carried out under the guidance of a meditation master in a comfortable sitting position and in a quiet place.

1. The mind focuses on the rising and falling of the abdomen. Breathing in, you notice the rising, breathing out, the falling, without considering the form of the abdomen or the words "rising" and "falling." Concentration is on the actual momentary process.

2. Spiritual emotions appearing during 1. are observed at the moment they appear. A memory is registered as a memory, a consideration as a consideration, a digression from the focus on the rising and falling of the abdomen as a digression. The emotion is followed to its disappearance, in order then to return to the actual exercise.

3. After a while, tiredness sets in. This, too, is to be observed: The arm's stiffness, the flesh tired of sitting. Neither rejection nor acceptance is the appropriate response. Experience has shown that these unpleasant feelings will disappear without any further assistance; otherwise the position should be changed. If the position of the leg is changed, then the change should be registered and executed with mindfulness, in order to turn again to the rising and falling of the abdomen. Pain itself, occurring intermittently, will disappear after a while of patiently observing its quality and the afflicted part of the body. Other-

wise, pain can be dissipated by changing the position or by interrupting the exercise—whereby these acts are again to be registered as change or interruption. With increasing experience, such pains can be controlled and eventually will no longer occur. Do not be discouraged by the many acts and thoughts that escape notice. It is important to persevere in the effort for perfection of perception. Once again, back to the rising and falling of the abdomen. Finally, you can turn your attention to the pauses between inhalation and exhalation, which, depending on one's position, can be noticed in lying or sitting.

4. The meditation exercises performed so far may feel disappointing; they take up a lot of time and bring no quick apparent success. Disappointment must also be noticed impartially; the same goes for doubts about the rightness of the way or feelings of happiness over an accomplished exercise. When these feelings recede, it is time to turn the spirit again attentively to the rising and falling of the abdomen.

The time allotted for such "clear-sighted meditation" should take up at least a day. The advanced student will not be tired out by such practice: On the contrary, it will enable her or him to continue meditation through the night, the next day, and still longer. Through the practice of mindfulness, the body can be directed and controlled and therefore can be removed from suffering. And the dissolution of suffering is the goal of Buddhism.

The 14th Dalai Lama destroys the colored powder from which a Kalachakra mandala was created as the conclusion of an initiation ceremony.

## Mysterious nirvana

The simple word, nirvana (or—in the Pali texts—nibbana), denotes the highest aim of Buddhists and has spawned more speculation than any other concept in the teachings of the Buddha. The word derives from a root meaning "to stop blowing," "to extinguish, or become extinct." It denotes the end of the cycle of rebirths, liberation from the force of death governing all of life.

What exactly does nirvana mean, the Buddha was often asked by his monks. He liked to answer with a paradox, as in *Undana VIII*: "I proclaim to you a non-coming and going, a non-standing firm and passing, freedom from rebirth; a non-standing still and a non-going on. There is no reason to desire life. This is the end of suffering." At another point the Buddha chose an analogy for existence and its extinction: Wind, blowing over a body of water, produces waves, thereby creating an illusion of masses of water hurrying along, but the image passes as soon as the wind dies down.

Because language is itself one of the aggregates, or groups, of existence, it is not a suitable medium for expressing what lies beyond. Language can, however, be used to formulate what nirvana is not; through rigorous negative characterization, we can approach the content of this mysterious concept: A "non-being," as the Buddha most concisely described it.

On the surface of the water the last traces of the mandala disappear.

Before death extinguishes the groups of existence, an Awakened One will have extinguished passions during his or her life. The Eightfold Path to this end, the Fourth of the Noble Truths describes, creates a far clearer image of nirvana than can be gained through any formulation. As one frees oneself from the physical, the next task opens before him or her—to free oneself from the spirit and from its activity, and this in turn marks the beginning of a new task. Now one must free oneself from the feeling of happiness that ensues from the liberation from body and spirit. This continual letting go into the eternal is nirvana. So far the Buddha himself described it.

What remains is the Buddha's unanswered question: What, if anything, actually survives? In the circle of dependent origination, only an existence without a self can arise: How, then, can anything that does not exist, something without substance, experience liberation and enter nirvana? For hundreds of years, commentators and interpreters of the Buddha's teachings have occupied themselves with just this problem. Some of the early Buddhists concluded that all existence ceased with the liberation: Nirvana is therefore nothing, a void. Others, the Pudgalavadins ("Personalists"), rejected an essential point in the teachings and maintained that, beyond dependent origination, beyond any individual self, there was a connective consciousness that experienced nirvana. In about 200 AD, Nagarjuna (see page 78), a reformer from southern India, finally arrived at the insight that the question only exists for those who have not yet achieved liberation.

"Reality … is in fact a convention upheld by those who know nothing else. But therein lies another reality, in which the other disappears, in which the other is undermined: Unutterable, without dimensions, without form, contrast, or boundary. It cannot be grasped, but it can be experienced fully. A crossing or bridge vanishing from itself … A waning of waning. What is real about it is that everything real can be brought to wane step by step, according to a plan. No thing-word can embody this. Nirvana—"extinction"—is finally just an image for a procedure that dissolves itself. It is like a bridge whose supporting pillars are still visible, even though, on the far side, the bridge has vanished."

*Heinrich Zimmer,*
Yoga and Buddhism

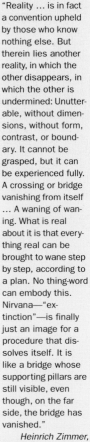

Worship of a stupa as a symbol for nirvana. Slate relief from Gandhara, 2nd/3rd c. AD.

The development of printing technique is closely connected to the expansion of Buddhism. Earlier than in other religious societies, holy texts as well as simple pictures—Buddha's footprints, for example—were multiplied to supply souvenirs for pilgrims and to encourage them to spread Buddhist teachings all over the world. The printing was done in wooden presses. Even a diamond-sutra with an exact date—May 11, 868—is preserved.

Buddhist manuscript from Nepal, 1686, with a depiction of the Buddha and the White Tara (see page 82).

### The problem of the canonical tradition

Whether the fundamental tenets described in the previous sections exactly summarize the crux of the Buddha's early teachings is open to question. We should be mindful that the Buddha's words have not been preserved as originally spoken. The teachings were probably first written down in the 3rd century BC under the Mauryan emperor Ashoka, but this text is no longer extant. Around this time Buddhism spread to the island of Lanka, as Ceylon (now Sri Lanka) was called in ancient times. At the bequest of a king about 200 years later, a complete canon was begun. Today, this text is still considered the most important source for research as well as for the followers of the early teachings. Pali, the scholarly Indian language chosen as vehicle, continues to dominate Buddhist writings, although the Buddha himself spoke Magadhi, and some surviving texts exist in Sanskrit and in other languages. The important concepts of the teachings exist in Sanskrit (for example, *dharma, sutra, nirvana*) as well as in Pali (for example, *dhamma, sutta, nibbana*).

Many inconsistencies in the canon can be traced to language problems, but the canon also contains formulations that most likely were not a part of the original teachings. Thus, for example, at one point thirst is called the origin of suffering; at another point, it is ignorance; the former can be eliminated through meditation, the latter through knowledge. In such discrepancies, the central problem of existence as well as the path to liberation, the Fourth of the Noble Truths, are called into question.

There are also a number of stylistic oddities; the striking repetitions, for example, produce an almost meditative effect. These

simplify memorization of texts, but make reading more laborious. In all likelihood, these repetitive elements did not come from the Buddha himself, whose contemporaries believed he was so successful in his mission specifically because of his personal language and oratory skills.

Two sutra scrolls (paper on wood) from the 12th c., Japan.

The canon we have today is known as the "Three Baskets" (*tripitaka*; Pali, *tipitaka*); each "basket" is a book. *Vinaya-pitaka*, the first of the books, contains the rules of discipline governing monastic life. There are about 230 rules that a monk must follow; breach of the rules has to be confessed. The *Vinaya-pitaka* also contains regulations concerning acceptance or exclusion from the monastic order. The book's contents seem in large part the same as the monastic rules laid down in the Third Council under the Emperor Ashoka.

The *Sutta-pitaka*, the "basket of the teachings," explains the actual teachings, mainly the sermons of the Buddha. It is divided into four collections (*nikaya*), into which the sermons were ordered according to stylistic criteria, mainly by their length. The *Sutta-pitaka* includes a copious appendix of many poems and birth stories (*jatakas*) relating the legends of the Buddha's supposed 550 earlier lives (see illus. page 163).

The third and latest book, the *Abhidhamma-pitaka*, addresses metaphysical, moral, and philosophic questions. Probably begun under Ashoka, it swelled to immense proportions in later centuries. The *Abidhamma* contains interpretations of the Buddha's sermons by learned scholars. One of these scholars was Buddhaghosha, a hermit living on Sri Lanka in the 5th century. Buddhaghosha was said to have written down his insights on so many palm leaves that he finally had no more living space and had to leave his cave. Interestingly enough, a German monk Nyanatiloka translated and wrote a commentary on the Buddhaghosha's extensive work, the "Path of Cleanliness" (see page 180).

### The origins of Buddhism

Many reports of the Buddha's missionary success have been preserved over the millennia; their tone is euphoric and their reliability dubious. The Buddha's original teachings were neither easy to understand nor comfortable to follow. They offered the laity no direct path to liberation and said nothing about the familiar and revered gods. Most likely the masses remained under the influence of Brahmanism and popular beliefs. It seems more probable that the Buddha's teachings were not thought of as a religion in the beginning, but as a philosophy aimed at a small circle of scholars concerned with the problem of liberation and awakening. And this is what they were to remain for hundreds of years after the death of the Master.

The surprising transformation of Buddhism into a world religion went hand in hand with political changes. The empire of Magadha, the Buddha's native region, had already become the greatest power in northern India under various dynasties during the 4th century BC. When Alexander the Great reached the Indus in 327, his counterpart King Poros was a strong leader, able to arrest the advancement of the Greeks. A few years after this confrontation of

Alexander the Great riding against Darius III. Mosaic from the *House of the Faun* in Pompeii, ca. 1st C. BC.

East and West, the first Maurya emperor ascended the throne in Pataliputra, the capital of Magadha. His grandson was Ashoka (reigned 268–232 BC), who expanded his kingdom to encompass the entire subcontinent and is still celebrated today as the first emperor of all of India. Perhaps one of the most remarkable of Ashoka's actions as emperor was that he proclaimed nonviolence a fundamental tenet of his kingdom.

Ashoka's predecessors had consolidated their power through an infamous secret service and Ashoka himself had been extremely brutal in his conquests, but after his last great battle, he found his way—according to his own report—to purification and to the teachings of the Buddha. Most likely, though, he had political motives for his proclamation of nonviolence. Although successful, he was unbeloved among his subjects, and once he had secured the outer boundaries of his kingdom, he turned his attention to internal security. Through the Buddha's morally demanding but humane teachings, which must have embodied an ideal held by many people, Ashoka was able to promote unity in his empire, offering the distant peoples of southern India some basis for identification with Magadha. Naturally, the difficult teachings would have had to be simplified into readily understandable fundamental tenets if they were to be politically effective. Ashoka therefore essentially promulgated his own ideas, based on the Buddha's words, but directed toward establishing and maintaining internal peace and protecting the wealth of the ruling classes. His basic tenets were respect for authority, nonviolence, moderation in the desire for wealth, and exact knowledge of and obedience to ethical duties. Whoever obeyed these rules was promised a most fortunate reincarnation for his or her next existence.

In order to publicize this simple but obviously effective state religion Ashoka had edicts carved into

Famous lion capital of the Ashoka pillar (see page 8) from Sarnath, north India. According to Buddhist interpretations, the animals in relief, appearing above the lotos shaft alternately with the Wheel of the Sun (also interpreted as the Wheel of the Teachings), embody birth, decay, sickness and death. The entire work reflects in its iconography and artistry the influence of the Achaemenid Persians.

Stupa III in Sanchi, north India. The burial mound with gate from the 1st c. BC housed the ashes of the Buddha's favorite pupils Shariputra and Maudgalyayana according to the inscription on the reliquary container.

After the earthly remains of the Buddha had been burned, his ashes, bones, and teeth were buried under reliqiary mounds. One eye-tooth, originally belonging to the king of Kalinga, somehow made its way to Anuradhapura on the island of Lanka in the 4th c. The rulers there often changed capitals and took the tooth with them on every move, until it

pillars and rocks along the most important roads, at pilgrimage shrines, and in centers of trade, and these edifices themselves soon became objects of sightseeing. Thus, the politically pious words were eagerly read and disseminated by word of mouth.

Ashoka then ordered seven of the eight reliquary hills housing the Buddha's ashes to be opened (see page 21) and the remains redistributed supposedly over 84,000 different hills throughout his kingdom. These *stupas* (see page 152) in turn increasingly became centers for Buddha worship and, together with this cult, the first Buddhistic rituals emerged. Ashoka also encouraged lay believers to go on pilgrimages to the places where Gautama had been active and erected monasteries for the previously homeless monks. With the building of the monasteries, Buddhist art began; this was bound to influence how the monks thought of themselves. Now that the monks' missionary work, formerly one of their primary duties, had been taken over by the state, and their economic needs were being met, the monks could turn their attention to scholarly activities. When this system broke down, with the fall of the Maurya dynasty in around 187 BC, the monasteries were obliged to seek private patronage (see page 57); this, again, changed the nature of the monastic order, but it also helped forge a closer alliance between the monks and the laity.

It was during Ashoka's reign that the Buddha's teachings became the religion Buddhism and spread beyond the boundaries of the Ganges valley. The emperor even sent emissaries into neighboring countries, and there, too, Buddhism found followers. The Buddha's insights and teachings traveled over the ancient trading routes as far as the Middle East and Greece.

### Teachings and schools

In a famous episode out of the Pali Canon (see page 46) some monks ask the Buddha about a group of Brahmans who were continually in such heated arguments over matters of philosophy that their discussions often turned into physical confrontations. Instead of defending one or the other of the Brahmans, as the monks had expected he would do, the Buddha related a parable: There was once a king who ordered his servant to bring an elephant before all those in the city who had been born blind. The servant allowed some of the blind to touch the trunk of the elephant, others the ears, others the feet, yet others the tusks. The king later asked the blind men what the animal looked like; each offered comparisons that concerned the one part he had touched, and the descriptions of the blind men conflicted drastically with one another. It was not possible to mediate or resolve their dispute because all of them lacked a complete view of the animal.

The Buddha surely recognized the "blindness" not only among the Brahmans but among his own monks as well. He repeatedly reminded them that arguments about details, by encouraging conflict, actually distracted from the real goal. This was one of the fundamental insights of the teachings, and, after the Master's death, it became the leading spiritual tenet (see page 29). Nevertheless, naturally enough, individuals came

finally ended up in Kotte. The Portuguese transferred the tooth to Goa, where the archbishop had it ground to powder and burned. Buddhist interpretation has it that at the time only an imitation of the tooth was abducted and destroyed. In 1603 the Dalada Maligawa temple in Kandy was built over the "real tooth of Buddha." The relic itself, or rather another copy of it, is carried through the streets of the city every year in July and August in a big procession.

along with their own qualities and ways of thinking and formulated their own specific versions of the original teaching.

Among the most important of the Buddha's followers there were always divergent camps, or schools, pursuing different directions. Maudgalyayana, for example, endeavored to develop his occult powers through the practice of mindfulness and meditation. Shariputra (see photo page 24), on the other hand, sought to attain the highest wisdom for himself, and a comprehensible formulation of the teachings for the laity. This nearly led to the founding of a separate school in which wisdom was equated with the way of simple faith and virtue—an interpretation that was to assume great importance in later years. In early Hinduism, the concept of *bhakti*, the loving devotion to a divinity, offered a path to salvation for the masses, and this tenet would clearly influence the development of Buddhism (see page 70).

Shariputra (left) and the sorcerer-monk Maudgalyayana (right) in a schematic Nepalese block print depiction dating from the early 20th c.

It was the concern of both Maudgalyayana and Shariputra to develop their abilities in order to put them at the service of the teachings. The Buddha's disciple, Maha Kashyapa, on the other hand, used his powers for his own ends. A rigid ascetic, Kashyapa had already contradicted the Buddha's directives during the Master's lifetime. Later he inevitably came into opposition with Ananda, whose benevolent, tolerant nature was perhaps most like that of the Buddha himself. Maha Kashyapa presided over the First Council, held soon after the Buddha's death. His dominance at the time is some indication that the ascetics had taken over the leadership in the Buddhist community, even though the Buddha's favorite, Ananda (see page 24), was acknowledged as the authoritative advisor.

The fact that Rajagriha was chosen as the site for the Council indicates that Maha Kashyapa had formed an alliance with King Ajatashatru of Magadha. This, however, presupposes that the First Council actually took place and was not just a fiction of the Pali Canon, as is more likely the case. Whatever the truth may be, the event has symbolic significance. Such secular alliances have continued to play a part in the life of Buddhism; even today, they take on the form found on Sri Lanka, where leading monks have allied themselves with politicians against the Tamils emigrating from India.

Arguments about details, which the Buddha discouraged and which he sidestepped with a parable, nevertheless arose, in part because his teachings are difficult to understand and include concepts that beg for interpretation. Thus, early in the history of Buddhism, many different schools emerged; most, however, can be classified into two principle streams that have come to be known as the Lesser and the Great Vehicles.

### The School of the Elders and the Great Community

"My teachings are like a raft, made to use to cross over, but not made to hold on to." So began the Buddha's story of a man traveling through a country full of suffering and dangers, who finally arrived at a river and recognized that the end of his travails, his salvation, lay on the far shore. He built his own raft—an

Boat ride as symbol for the Buddhist passage.

Hinayana monk next to a Mahayana monk in Bodh Gaya.

image of the teachings—to carry him across. Then, as soon as he arrived on the other side, the raft lost all value for him and could be left behind for others, who still lingered in the same desperate straits.

The image of the teachings as a raft or vehicle, as a means to liberation with no inherent value, became common in discussions among Buddhist scholars— as an image, it has not escaped a certain amount of ridicule. Thus, at the Third Council, the "Representatives of the Great Community," the Mahasanghikas, held the opinion that the Elders' School of Wisdom offered too small a raft, or what they called a "Lesser Vehicle" (*hina yana*). The elders' teaching, however close it may have been to the Buddha's original teaching, could neither in theory nor in practice offer a means for saving all of humankind; rather, it could aid only a select few to cross over to the other shore. "Hinayana," thus, is a term of disparagement essentially attached to this stream of Buddhism by the later Mahayana, or "Great Vehicle" (see page 68). Followers of the early teaching therefore preferred to call themselves the "School of the Elders" (*theravada*), a term that is all the more appropriate because, as in former times, there were at least 17 different Hinayana schools besides the Theravadins.

Although they refused entry to almost no one, in theory at least giving everyone an opportunity to travel the path to liberation, the conflict at the Third Council plainly demonstrated that the Theravadins placed their own liberation above that of others. While the School of the Elders continued to think of the Buddha as a historical figure, they soon ascribed to him miraculous powers. Today, the followers of the Hinayana still consider themselves bound to the traditional texts and follow the monastic rules written down under the Emperor Ashoka. Theological speculation is discouraged, but there is a tendency toward the mystical that was already evident in the Buddha's disciple Maudgalyayana (see page 52). The mysterious nirvana (see page 44) has assumed the character of a paradise, as Ashoka popularized it, and the definition of the individual has also evolved: It has been endowed with a soul that can savor paradise, provided it has accumulated a good karman.

Comparatively little is known for certain about the philosophy of the Mahasanghikas, who opposed the School of the Elders in the councils; none of their own texts survive and the reports that have survived originated with their opponents, whose bias shows. It seems that the Mahasanghikas were instrumental in preparing the way for the claim that Gautama himself was only an unimportant incarnation of an original being, an Absolute. In dealing with the Mahayana in the next chapter, we will see how this idea smoothed the path to liberation for the masses.

Pre-historical Buddha Kashyapa depicted in a modern Nepalese block print. Kashyapa, the last of the pre-historical Buddhas, supposedly was born in the Deer Park in Sarnath, where the Buddha later held his famous first discourse.

Procession of Buddhist women. Painting from the 13th c. on the southern window of the Nandamanya temple in Pagan, Burma.

These new movements had already gained great momentum during the time of Ashoka. Among the bitter disputes between the streams was disagreement over the nature of the arhat. The Mahasanghikas pointed out that even sages have nocturnal emissions of semen, brought about in dreams through the temptation of Mara's daughters. They concluded therefore that no arhat had arrived at the level of liberation he might imagine he had attained.

Finally, the transcription of the teachings into a canon seems to have brought about a kind of stagnation. This is readily seen in the Buddhist attitude toward women. "Beware of women" the canon warns. "For every wise woman, there are a thousand that are either stupid or bad. A woman's character is more devious than the path taken by fish in the water. She is as wild as a robber and just as treacherous. Only rarely does she speak the truth: Lying and truth are the same to her." Because the Buddha himself had preached equality and had—supposedly at the urging of his stepmother—sanctioned the establishment of a cloister for nuns, we are loath to believe he would have demeaned himself with such outrageous statements. It is not unlikely that later generations took issue with the Buddha's conception of women and felt little compunction about tacking such judgments onto his sermons. Once written down and accepted into the canon, however, they assumed the air of authority and are still promulgated today.

### Hinayana today

**Sri Lanka**. One of the missionaries sent out by the Emperor Ashoka to the neighboring countries of India, was Mahinda, the son or brother of the emperor. In 250 BC Mahinda reached the island of Sri Lanka, in the Indian Ocean. Theravada/Hinayana Buddhism has survived here through today, relatively unaffected by the habits and culture of later invaders from India and Europe.

For the Buddha, his self-imposed homelessness was a deliberate act. He considered the sedentariness of

monks dangerous for it limited their contact with the world to the same people. Such continuity was likely to contribute to the growth of a community that would necessarily impose certain social duties that are not conducive to goals of monastic life. The home-bound monk, moreover, might begin to pay attention to his appearance and to worry about his property, concerns that would clearly conflict with Buddhist teachings.

In the beginning, the monks of Sri Lanka were homeless. They stayed in simple protective huts (*vihara*) only during the monsoon; these rough shelters were not too far from villages where they could continue to beg for alms and do missionary work, but far enough to allow them to carry on their meditation practices undisturbed. In time, these huts became the rudiments of monasteries, also called vihara. The Buddha's warnings, thus, were not ill-founded.

Within the monasteries, missionary work waned as pursuit of the personal path to salvation grew ever more important. The result was that the monks grew more isolated. At the same time, particularly through the bequests of kings, their wealth grew and, with it, their social status. The monasteries found themselves inevitably drawn into political entanglements. If the displeasure of the rulers threatened the monasteries' financial backing, the monks could hardly remain objective. The monasteries learned to teach only what would not offend. This unfortunate alliance between the spiritual and secular authorities determined the fate of Sri Lanka for hundreds of years, persisting even under British colonial rule, when the monasteries were dependent on the rich, mostly conservative families

Mihintale, birthplace of Buddhism on Sri Lanka and a center for pilgrimages.

Buddhist festivals on Sri Lanka: The holiday calendar is marked by the days of the full moon (*poya*). Every full and new moon, smaller festivities take place. In the nights of the full moon, processions visit the temples, flowers are sacrificed, incense is burned, and holy texts are recited. The full moon in May (*vesak*) as well as the full moon in June (*poson*) have a special meaning: Vesak is the festival of the Buddha's Awakening, birth, and death, while Poson recalls of Mahinda's mission in Sri Lanka. Apart from those festivals there are holidays of local importance, which commemorate supposed visits of the Buddha in a city.

Modern depiction of the Buddha in front of the town hall of Colombo, Sri Lanka.

Monk on Sri Lanka.

who also supported the colonial forces. In the colonial era, the caste system also entered the social structure of the monasteries, as benefactors would only allow members of their own class to be admitted into the vihara.

Such exclusionary practices, coupled with the effects of colonial rule, led over many years to the decline of monastic life on the island. Although monks from Burma and Thailand brought some new impulses to Sri Lankan Buddhism in the 18th century, a real Buddhist "renaissance" came about only when Europe "discovered" Buddhism. In 1891, the Mahabodhi Society was founded on Sri Lanka: From here, interested laity and ordained monks from the West were able to acquaint Europeans with the texts and the ideas of the Pali Canon.

Since the end of the 19th century, Sri Lanka's independence movement also helped fuel a revival of Buddhism as the teachings strengthened the insular national consciousness. But the new political weight did little to strengthen or elucidate older spiritual values. Contemporary political parties continue to adapt their tactics to the opinions of leading Buddhist circles, as monks openly support whichever faction promises them the greatest material gain. In 1972, the monks supported the socialists, who declared Buddhism Sri Lanka's state religion. In 1977, they did an about-face and supported the conservatives because the Left wanted to levy taxes on monastic institutions.

Neither the monks nor the lay believers of Sri Lanka seem to feel any discordance between the wish for liberation and such worldly machinations. The population at large, in any case, seems to have an extremely uncomplicated approach to Buddhistic teachings. They speak of "Lord Buddha," a higher being, enthroned in heaven, to whom they pray in a quite naive manner.

**Burma (Myanmar)**. There is evidence tracing the spread of the Hinayana back to the 5th century AD, when large parts of what was then called East Bengalia (and is today Bangladesh) were still an impenetrable wilderness. The teachings of the Buddha arrived here not overland but through the busy sea trade with the courts of West Bengalia and Orissa. The Mahayana appears to have gained a foothold only in the 9th century. It was never able to dominate due to continual suppression by the state, which sought cultural unity as a means to maintain political stability. There are some stories of a King of Pagan who attempted to elevate Theravada Buddhism to the status of a state religion in the 9th century, but that seems more legend than fact. Still, Burma maintained trade relations with Sri Lanka, and, over centuries of commerce, Sri Lanka became a kind of model of Theravada Buddhism that did have an influence on Buddhism's development in Burma. The Burmese variety of Theravada, however, also encompasses elements clearly stemming from popular cults and from Tantric Buddhism (see page 88); the latter probably came to Burma via Bengalia and remained popular into the 16th century.

In 1287 AD, Pagan was conquered by Mongolia and then destroyed in 1299 by Thai peoples, who established their capital in Pegu and proclaimed the Hinayana obligatory in 1479. After the oppressed Burmese won independence in the 16th century, they waged

"Buddhist" cavalry on a campaign. 19th c. depiction, Burma. Hostilities between Burma and Thailand peaked in the 18th c. when Burma presumed to "Buddhist imperialism" and tried to conquer first Thailand and Laos, and then, in the 19th c., also British India.

## Buddhism in Southeast Asia

**1st c. AD**
First trade ships sail from Kalinga (Orissa) in India to southeast Asia

**after 2nd c.**
First Buddhist communities in the Chinese north of Vietnam (Annam)

**after 224**
Rise of the Sassanids in Iran impede trade between India and the West; trade shifts to east and southeast Asia

**4th c.**
In central Vietnam the Hindu empire Champa develops under Indian influence

**5th c.**
Centers of Hinayana in Burma, oldest sources from Java and Sumatra

**ca. 550**
Funan, a Chinese satellite empire, divides into the empires of Cambodia and Dvaravati, the latter with first centers of Hinayana

**580**
Chinese school of Chan forms dependencies in northern Vietnam

**671–695**
Chinese monk I-ching travels India und Indonesia

**7th c.**
Mahayana and Tantra on Sumatra

**770–1095**
Pala dynasty in India, cultural exchange with southeast Asia

**8th c.**
Mahayana Buddhism in Cambodia and Java

**after 9th c.**
Mahayana in Pagan, Burma; the Khmer Empire rules over large parts of southeast Asia; apart from Hinduism, Mahayana spreads
**938**
Vietnam independent of China
**ca. 970**
Mahayana national religion in Vietnam
**after 11th c.**
Theravada Buddhism in Burma
**ca. 1150**
First Buddhist ruler in Angkor, Hinduism declines as a result
**1287**
Mongols conquer Pagan, Burma
**13th/14th c.**
Thai peoples from southern China spread to Thailand, Burma, and Laos, where they form small nations accepting Hinayana
**after 14th c.**
Buddhism on Sumatra replaced by Islam, on Java by Hinduism
**1407**
Troups of the Chinese Ming dynasty conquer Vietnam and destroy Buddhist sites
**1428**
After expulsion of the Chinese from Vietnam, Confucianism is introduced there and Buddhists are persecuted
**1431**
The Khmer capital Angkor destroyed by Thai peoples; the empire,

Monk at the famed Golden Stone at the Kyaiktiyo Pagoda, Burma.

war "in the name of Buddha" against their Thai neighbors. In the 18th century, the hostility between these two countries reached new heights, as Burma presumed to follow a path of "Buddhist imperialism," attempting to conquer first Thailand and Laos and then, in the 19th century, even British colonial India. When the British retaliated and annexed parts of Burma, a profound crisis in the unity of the Buddhist order erupted. In 1868, a Fifth Buddhist Council was convened in Mandalay; its goal was again to lay down the canon in written form. The effect was to strengthen the sense of community, and this finally helped bring Burma's struggle for independence to a successful conclusion.

Burma (today Myanmar) has been independent since 1948. At first, the state attempted to bring about a kind of synthesis between Buddhism and socialism: The fundamental evils named in the teachings—greed, hatred, and blindness—were attributed to capitalistic thinking, and a nirvana on earth was supposed to lie in economic equality. When military forces overthrew the government in 1962, this daring goal was also shattered and a harsh military dictatorship hostile to foreign influence—albeit in the name of Buddhism—was established. Monks have continued to play an active part in the resistance to the military's despotic atrocities, though, we ought to note, their motives were not always spiritually pure or humanitarian in nature. For instance, the monks sought to have the nationalization of companies revoked, since by this process they had lost their greatest source of income, private benefactors.

**Thailand**. In the Thai kingdom of Dvaravati, the Hinayana was known since around the middle of the 6th century. The teaching began to spread, particularly in the 13th century, when Thai tribes from southern China advanced into Thailand, Laos, and Burma where they established several small Buddhist states (Sukhothai, Lannathai, and Ayutthaya were in Siam, Pegu was in Burma, and Lan Chang was Laos). The political and spiritual leadership resided in Ayutthaya, which therefore became the target of Burmese military actions in the 16th century (see above.) After the danger had been at

Temple buildings of the ancient royal capital Ayutthaya, Thailand, destroyed in 1767.

from then on called Kampuchea, adopts Theravada
**1471**
Fall of Champa
**1479**
Under a Thai king the Sri Lankan monastic rules become general law in Burma
**1592**
Ayutthaya shakes off Burmese rule (since 1569) and becomes a center of Theravada
**16th c.**
Vietnam divided into northern and southern halves, both kingdoms, though enemies, propagate Buddhism again
**1707**
Laos divided into several small empires where animistic cults dislodge Buddhism
**1767**
Ayutthaya destroyed by Burmese; decline of the Siam Empire creates crisis for Buddhism in Thailand
**1802**
Vietnam unified under one emperor, new blossom of Buddhism in the northern part of the country
**1804–1868**
Prince Mongkut reforms Buddhism in Thailand
**1824–1826, 1852**
Burma wages two wars against British India
**1841**
Kampuchea annexed by Vietnamese, Khmer culture suppressed; numerous Buddhist temples destroyed

**1857–1867**
Southern Vietnam occupied by French, Buddhism declines

**1863**
Kampuchea becomes French protectorate

**1868–1871**
Fifth Buddhist Council in Mandalay, revision and renewal of the old canon

**1883–1884**
French occupy northern Vietnam as well

**1887**
French colonies and protectorates unified (called Indochina)

**1893**
Laos becomes part of Indochina

**after 1920**
Buddhist renaissance movement in Vietnam turns into main motor of the opposition against the French

**1940**
Japan conquers Vietnam

**1945**
French struggle to regain colonial suppremacy, arrests of Buddhist monks who are considered politically suspicious

**1946**
Beginning of the First Indochina War

**1948**
Buddhist Socialism in independent Burma

**1953**
End of the French protectorate over Kampuchea, attempt to imitate Burmese politics; communists ("Khmer Rouge") lose influence

Temple area of Wat Phra Keo, Bangkok. Slender, tapering chedi are typical for Thai sacred architecture; they represent a regional version of the basic stupa form.

least temporarily fended off in 1592, Theravada Buddhism in Siam experienced a cultural flowering that only ended in 1767 when Burma again conquered Ayutthaya. This time, the capital was completely destroyed, the kingdom dismantled, and the people sought refuge in the deities of local cults. At the beginning of the 19th century, a profound reformation of the Hinayana took place through the efforts of Prince Mongkut, who also introduced Christian elements into Thai Buddhism. Another conspicuous feature of the Hinayana in Thailand is the reverence for the king; this grew out of certain Chinese and Indian traditions that have been used by local rulers for their own purposes well into the present day. The state has repeatedly tried to gain control over the affairs of the monks and has succeeded more than once in misusing Buddhism for political aims. One such instance is the manipulation of the widespread belief in Thailand in the imminent coming of the kingdom of Maitreya (see page 12): Government reforms or national strikes have been justified on religious grounds as preparing the way for the birth of the savior.

**Laos.** Whereas many monks in Thailand gave their support to the anticommunist propaganda during the Vietnam War, the order in Laos backed the communist Pathet Lao. This is proof, once again, that in all of the Hinayana countries today, Buddhism plays an active political role, generally favoring whichever party promises greater affluence and greater freedom. Unfortunately, the gamble did not pay off in Laos.

Laos was the last of the original Thai states to accept the Hinayana in about 1356. During the 18th century, it reverted almost totally to its local cult deities, but then returned to Buddhism in 1893 when Laos became a French protectorate. The Hinayana served as the driving force of the resistance movement against foreign domination. When the French withdrew from Laos in 1945, pro-American military rulers came into power and began to curtail the rights of self-administration of the orders. This explains the monasteries' sympathy toward the communists. However, when the latter took over the government in 1975, they too introduced measures that curtailed the seemingly all too influential sangha. Buddhism in Laos has won more freedom and its standing has improved since the period of national-communist isolation passed and the borders to neighboring Buddhist Thailand opened once again.

Gate of Angkor Thom in the middle of the Cambodian jungle. Engraving from 1868.

**1954**
French troops leave Indochina; independent nations Laos, Cambodia, Northern and Southern Vietnam are born
**1954–1956**
Sixth Council in Rangoon, decision to send Buddhist missionaries all over the world
**1955**
U.S. starts military aid for South Vietnam
**1964**
Beginning of Second Indochina War
**1970**
Sihanouk regime in Cambodia overturned by pro-American military; civil war
**1973**
Last U.S. troops leave Southern Vietnam
**1975**
Communists rule in Vietnam, Laos, and Cambodia; the Khmer Rouge try to extirpate Buddhism; reprisals against Buddhists also in Vietnam
**1979**
Vietnamese victory over the Khmer Rouge
**1987**
Vietnamese government tolerant toward Buddhism
**1989**
Vietnamese troops leave Cambodia; here, too, life becomes easier for Buddhists
**1991**
End of the Soviet Union: Buddhist revival in many formerly communist nations of southeast Asia

An apsaras, a heavenly nymph, as characteristically depicted in both Hinduism and Buddhism. Flat relief from Angkor, Cambodia.

**Cambodia**, once a part of the enormous Khmer kingdom (from the 9th to the 13th century), was not one of the original Hinayana states. Quite the contrary: For centuries, Hinduism was widely accepted here, followed by the Mahayana. But, in the 13th century, the Thai peoples began to weaken the kingdom, and the weight of their influence also meant that the old school of wisdom came to dominate. This school bore the colorings of the Thai people; for example, it tended to place all hopes on the future Buddha Maitreya to eliminate wrongs. From a political point of view, Kampuchea, as the country has been called since the capital was moved from Angkor to Phnom Penh in the 15th century, has never been able to free itself from its unenviable position between Thailand and Vietnam. This geographic vulnerability led the people of Cambodia either to seek new alliances for protection or to seek refuge in religion, whether Christian or Moslem.

Buddhism first suffered severe reprisals in Cambodia in 1841, when the country was occupied by the Vietnamese who wanted to destroy the entire Khmer culture. It became a French protectorate in 1863, and embarked upon a relatively peaceful century during which Cambodia remained largely untouched by world events and an orthodox form of Theravada flourished. Nevertheless, the monks took part in the resistance movement, and the French were finally ousted in 1953. Prince Sihanouk then hoped to establish a kind of Buddhist socialism, as in Burma, and suppressed the radical left or "Khmer Rouge." In the meantime, pro-American military leaders who sided with South Vietnam staged a coup and overthrew the government in 1970. The ensuing civil war between them and the Khmer Rouge ended in 1975 with the victory of the communists. Under the Khmer Rouge regime, many Buddhists were murdered—their way of life was considered hostile to the ideals of the radical left. Then, in 1979, Vietnam defeated the Khmer Rouge. The political chaos that ensued and the corresponding crisis of the Theravada in Cambodia were only ended by the intervention of the United Nations and the reinstatement of Sihanouk as chief of state.

The Buddhist communities in Burma, Thailand, Laos, and Cambodia are large and often very influential, but there are also miserable, desperately impoverished Hinayana enclaves in southeastern **Bangladesh** as well as in the vicinity of some Buddhist shrines in **India**. Their survival in both political and social terms, is highly uncertain.

Overgrown and deserted: Sacred Buddhist buildings in Cox's Bazaar, Bangladesh.

At the end of the 19th century, it became clear that lay organizations played a far more dynamic role in the Buddhist movement on Sri Lanka than did the community of monks. This is largely because most monks do not enter the monastery out of conviction, in answer to a "call," or because it is their over-riding desire; indeed, it is usually not their own but their parents' decision. Usually, it is the young-est son of a family who is sent to the monastery, somewhere between the ages of eight and ten. Often he comes from an ordinary family, has no particular prospects for a sec-ular career, or a fortune-teller has prophesied a bad future for him.

Under such circumstances, it is no easy task to live according to monastic rule, especially when celi-bacy is required and no personal property is allowed. Such a decision can only be made by a mature adult who has examined himself carefully. In terms of formalities, there is no real barrier to leaving the monast-ery—monks are in any case asked once a year whether and why they still want to belong to the order. But leaving the monastery is risky: The young monks have no profession, and their general education is far below the standard of public schools. Their chance of finding a place in society is poor. And, should they later decide to return to the mon-astery, they would have to reenter on the lowest level of the hierarchy.

What we should understand is that the community of monks is not a union of highly spiritual or learned men. Of course, there is great scholarliness, but it resides alongside considerable stupidity and the rote repetition of monastic rules. Strength of character is found next to petty opportunism, awakened asceticism next to greed.

Despite these personal differ-ences in character, all monks share in a routine that regulates the course of daily life. After breakfast at six in the morning, they are sent to col-lect alms. At noon, they have their last meal of the day. This is fol-lowed by spiritual education, which can mean anything from mere repetition to the highest steps of meditation.

Just as the monks can hardly be seen as a homogeneous body, so their living quarters diverge radically in quality. The 5000 monasteries of Sri Lanka may own large tracts of land and have ample monetary means, but their wealth is not divided equally. In some monast-eries, four or five elderly men may eke out a miserable existence, while in others the monks may bask in a surprising amount of splendor.

Three different sects have been established on Sri Lanka. They are distinct from one another less in their teachings than in their social attitudes (see page 50f.). Kandy, a provincial city, proudly houses one of the Buddha's teeth, which is

Colorful, naive murals in a contemporary Buddhist temple in Matara, Sri Lanka. Such ensembles are didactic pictorial introductions to the Buddhist imaginative world.

promenaded through the streets in a spectacular procession once a year. It is also the seat of the Siam Nikaya. This order was founded during the 18th century by Thai monks in response to the increasingly mundane interests of other Buddhists. But despite its revivalist origin, its members are drawn exclusively from the upper classes and they publicly declared their allegiance to the caste system. In the early 19th century, a counter-reaction appeared in the form of the Amarapura Nikaya, a sect influenced by Burma, whose main center lies in the small city of Galle in the south. A few years later in l835, the Ramanya Nikaya was formed near Colombo, in response to what it claimed was the materialism of the other two sects. The Ramanya Nikaya adopted as their symbol the palm leaf, which they use instead of the umbrella of the colonial rulers to keep themselves dry.

Buddhism on Sri Lanka suffered the most serious setback in its history during the 17th century. At that time, the nuns' cloisters, which had not been reformed in the religious revival, disappeared. Thus, about 3000 "Eight Precepts Women," who live according to the rule of the sangha, were stripped of their official status. Since then, they have not been permitted to attend the Buddhist university and there is little hope that the patriarchs dominating monastic life on Sri Lanka today will rethink their positions.

### Return to the divine

The Buddha taught that all brooding over the existence and activity of the gods only obscures the path to liberation. Still, his followers felt free to populate and embellish their individual pantheons in order to make the teachings more readily understandable. This does not mean that they generated a simplified vision of the cosmos, as many have argued. On the contrary, the inevitable theological speculations of later Buddhism led to a very complex and demanding world view whose beginnings can be traced back to the order of the Mahasanghikas (see page 54) in northwestern India 2000 years ago.

The desire of lay believers to clothe transcendental ideas in concrete forms was not the only reason for the fundamental transformation of Buddhist teachings. In political terms, the collapse of the Mauryan empire forced the monasteries, which had by then grown accustomed to receiving state support, to seek new patrons. The monks therefore cultivated connections with financially strong lay circles, who in turn expected to find paths to liberation that would not conflict with their worldly dealings. In any case, the arhats, who concerned themselves primarily with the fate of the individual, were the target of increasing criticism. The teachings themselves, critics pointed out, had rejected individualism: The arhats, though seemingly unaware of any contradiction in terms or of any inconsistencies, nevertheless were vulnerable to charges of nurturing the individual, even of egotism. From a philosophical point of view, their path to salvation was paved with contradictions.

Could a human being follow the Buddha's path on his or her own strength? Or was it only possible for a higher being to walk between so many tensions and contradictions, without intentionally or unintentionally siding with one or the other of the competing powers? Was it perhaps only possible for human beings to free themselves from the dilemma of life through devotion to the higher being? Surely,

A noble lay believer, perhaps, Prince Vessantara, worshipping the Buddha. Mural from the 3rd c. AD from Miran, Turkestan, a caravan center in central Asia. The worshiper's clothing reveals the peculiarities of the Gandharan style; the prince is seated on the throne in European fashion.

resignation played a great role in these questions; in fact, Buddhism was no stranger to pessimistic views.

Even the Hinayana, the followers of the Elders' School of Wisdom, could not deny that the conditions of life had deteriorated considerably since the Buddha's lifetime. No one seemed any longer to be in a position to walk the path to nirvana described in the authentic teachings. After the miracle of the Awakening, earthly existence had again of necessity sunk into the quagmire of wars and epidemics. Human life expectancy had become shorter; finally, when life consisted of only a few short years, a period of renewal could begin, leading ever so slowly to a new climax. This climax is promised to come at the end of millions of years in the form of the incarnation of the Buddha-to-come, Maitreya.

These ways of thought found acceptance among the Hinayana only a few centuries after the death of the Buddha, but they form an essential part of the Mahayana. It is therefore not surprising that the hostility between these two schools that had overshadowed the Councils began slowly to disappear. Reports by Chinese pilgrims (see page 131) substantiated that, in some Buddhist monasteries in India, the more numerous followers of the Hinayana lived and taught together with the followers of Mahayana under one roof.

The Mahayana conception of the divine was not based on the gods of popular folklore, who were revered by lay believers of both schools. The Mahayana turned, rather, to the figure of the Buddha. They projected onto him concepts drawn from the Brahman pantheon. The Teaching of the Three Bodies,

Xuan-zang (7th c.), one of the most famous Chinese Buddhist pilgrims, returned from India with numerous text scrolls on his shoulders. The fly swatter in his left hand symbolizes the readiness to ward off evil spirits, the tiger at his side, the pilgrim's firm resolution to fight for the new teachings. Above left the Buddha sits enthroned on a lotos. Depiction on a silk scroll from Dunhuang, China.

which became the basis for a complex system of Buddha incarnations, was also borrowed from Brahmanism. According to this teaching, a body of the Absolute (*dharmakaya*) exists in nirvana; it is the highest form, in which all Buddhas are identical with one another. At the middle level is a transcendental body (*sambhogakaya*), the personification of Truth,

that can be perceived not with the senses but with the spirit only. This is the other-worldly Buddha who, filled with wisdom and compassion, embodies the actual god of salvation. But, in order to disseminate the teachings and to lead people on the correct path, the transcendental body takes on a visible body (*nirmanakaya*), the "body of transformation," in this world, as was the case with Siddhartha Gautama and as will be the case in the future with Maitreya. The spiritual superiority of these visible beings should not obscure the fact that they are human and therefore not to be revered: They are able to teach but not to redeem in themselves.

Tibetan lay believer prostrating himself as an expression of his submission. "Pious pilgrims sometimes measure the circular walk around pilgrimage sites or pilgrimage routes around such sacred places as Mount Kailash with their own body by placing their prayer cord on the head each time before they arise from their prostrate position. They then walk these few steps and again prostrate themselves. Days, even weeks can pass in this fashion, the spirit firmly fixed on the numinous." (K.-H. Everding)

The hope of mankind is therefore directed toward the sambhogakaya. Believers need not expect insights and self-discipline to lead to this body; instead, the basis of liberation lies in the transcendent Buddha's intention to redeem. Human beings need only express their humility or devotion—through prayer, reverence of a Buddha image, or by calling on the Perfected—in order to enjoy the grace of the transcendent Buddha. This loving devotion, in Hinduism known as *bhakti,* was instrumental on all paths to liberation developed by Indian philosphers during the first centuries AD. Whoever practiced bhakti and lived a pure life in words, thoughts, and deeds would be rewarded with awakening in the next world. The Mahayana thus juxtaposed the belief in human misery with the belief in the transcendent power of the Buddha. Belief in the self, the "egotism" of the Hinayana, was thus drastically limited. The

extinction of the self, the highest aim of the Elders'
School of Wisdom was now to be attained through
faith in the divine, not through faith in personal
strength.

Naturally enough, the redemptive power of the
sambhogakaya was subject to particular complex
interpretation. The transcendental body, *jina* or
*dhyanibuddha* as it had been called earlier,
was envisaged as the ruler over the Buddha-
lands (*buddha-ksetra*). He admitted believers to
his kingdom, a kind of intermediate paradise, from
which the crossing into nirvana first became
possible. This idea introduced a new quality
into the older teachings, wherein the ascent
had been depicted as a series of steps: Now
a person need only complete the step to the
gate of the Buddha-land by declaring his
devotion to a higher Compassion; after his
entrance, he would be prepared for
liberation by the higher being.

The qualities of the Buddha-lands were
described precisely in order to give believers a good
picture of the blessings offered by the intermediate
paradise. Descriptions ranged from the climate to
the virtues of the people in the transcendental
kingdom; they even included the promise that here
women would be reborn as men. Extremely naive
and inescapably dictated by the moral values of the
times, this picture-book world plainly revealed the
subservience of the majority of the Mahayana Buddhists to the principle of divinity. To deal effectively
with different qualities, several Buddha-lands were
imagined, some pure and unmarred, others replete
with blemishes and worries, such as the land of the
Buddha Shakyamuni—the world in which we live.

Initially, the only important Buddhas were Amitabha in the kingdom Sukhavati, who was revered
especially in Japan (where he was known as Amida)
and in China (see page 141), and Akshobhya, the ruler
of the kingdom Abhirati, who was revered in India.

Outline of the Buddhist cosmos:

1 World mountain Meru
2 Seven concentric mountain ranges and oceans
3 Salt sea
4 Subsidiary mountain range
5 Continent of Paravideha
6 Continent of Iambud-vipa, the human world
7 Continent of Aparaqodanya
8 Continent of Uttarakatu
9 Palace of the Brahma
10 Devaloka, the realm of the lower gods and fabled beings
11 Rupadhatu, the heavenly spheres of pure form
12 Arupadhatu, the spheres of transcendental formlessness.

Amitabha, "the Infinite Light," one of the transcendent Buddhas, enthroned with an alms bowl in his hands in the western Buddha-land Sukhavati. Detail from a Tibetan picture scroll (*thangka*).

Sukhavati was located in the west of the Buddha cosmos, Abhirati in the east (Indian geographers placed east at the top of their maps, rather than north, as is conventional today). Later, in Tantrism (see page 100), other Buddhas were added: The four cardinal directions as well as the center became occupied.

During the 6th century, the Buddha occupying the center became the personification of the Absolute, as Adibuddha, so that the dharmakaya (see page 70), who had until then been unrecognizable also took on shape. At the beginning this central spot in the Buddhist cosmos belonged to Vairocana (and for the Buddhists of East Asia, he kept it), but the Indian believers gave his place to Vajrasattva.

The bodhisattvas were also reinterpreted in this system. Because of their far-sightedness and their wisdom, they (like the historic Buddha) were still considered legitimate "candidates for Awakening" who sacrificed their personal liberation in order to benefit the rest of humanity. In Mahayana Buddhism, the desire to attain a better Buddha-land in a later existence and pass from there into nirvana was surpassed by the desire to become such a bodhisattva. These beings, of course, also occupied Buddha-lands. The most important bodhisattvas were Avalokiteshvara, "The Lord Who is Seen," and Manjushri, "The Buddha's Wisdom." The former is of exalted goodness, the latter is especially wise.

**Akshobhya**: Carries the symbols of firmness; as a transcendant Buddha, he touches the earth with his right hand, while he holds the *vajra* (thunderbolt, symbol of the eternal); as ruler of the Buddha-land Abhirati, though, he carries an alm bowl in his left and the vajra is part of the fundaments of his throne where also his symbolic animal, the elephant, can be found; in colored representations, Akshobhya is blue-black.

**Amitabha**: Symbolizes longevity; as a transcendant Buddha he is represented in the pose of meditation similar to the images of the historical Buddha, in colored illustrations, Amitabha is red, Gautama, on the other hand, golden; as ruler of the Buddha-land Sukhavati, Amitabha holds the alm bowl in his hand, on the pedestal of his throne, the lotos flower (purity) and his symbolic animal, the peacock, are shown.

**Amoghasiddhi**: Signifies encouragement, expressed in the gesture of promised protection (*abhayamudra*), his attribute in one hand being the double vajra (not on all illustrations), Amoghasiddhi is connected to the element water and is often protected by a snake (symbolizes humidity of the ground), he is mounted on Garuda, his symbolic color is green.

**Ratnasambhava**: Gestures of the right hand for charity (*varadamudra*), in his left he carries the jewel *cintamani* which fulfills all wishes; he is mounted on a horse, symbolic color is gold.

**Vairocana**: Gesture of teaching (*dharmachakramudra*), in his hand he holds the sun disk; occasionally he is represented with four faces (being in the center, he sees in all four directions and thus is omniscient), mounted on a lion, symbolic color is white.

**Vajrasattva** and **Vajradhara**: Carrying an ornament with five points on his head, his right hand in front of his chest holds the vajra, symbol of the eternal, of nirvana and the male principle, in his left hand next to his hip carries a bell (*ghanta*) symbolizing the transient, the samsara, and the female principle, symbolic color is white; Vajradhara carries the same attributes, but his hands are crossed and his symbolic color is blue-black.

The transcendent Buddha Amoghasiddhi (above), lord over the Buddha-land of the north, has his right hand raised in a gesture promising protection (*abhayamudra*; see page 171). Vajrasattva (below) is lord over all natural laws and indirectly the lord of all the Buddha-lands, as the Absolute is embodied in him. Contemporary Nepalese block prints.

The Bodhisattva Padmapani. Fragment of a gold bronze, Gyantse, central Tibet, 16th c. The "Lotos holder"—thus the literal translation of the name Padmapani—compassionately supports believers on their way to redemption.

### New ways to liberation

Belief in liberation through faith in god offered easy access to Buddhist teachings. Such a belief did away with the restrictive view that limited liberation to a narrow path for a select few. The "new Buddhism" was plainly a "large vehicle," able to carry many people.

The basic idea of the Mahayana—the path of self-liberation as promulgated in the old school of wisdom—no longer seemed to offer a practical alternative; it was far better for the believer to place his or her trust in foreign help. Three important considerations were cited to justify this theory. First, it had become a widely accepted postulate that a transcendent Buddha was superior to anything earthly, but that a part of his being was found in everything mortal. Thus every individual is capable of liberation, and can justly hope to enter nirvana. The second consideration arose from the inter-dependency of people: Karman could no longer be deduced merely from the good or bad actions of an individual; instead, since actions are usually a part of, or a reaction against, the actions of others, all are responsible for the karman. Greater solidarity in this life was therefore critical for the hereafter; this opened up the possibility that spiritual merits or debts might be transferred. But, since people unfortunately usually have more vices than virtues to distribute, a third postulate seemed necessary: The bodhisattvas became the greatest bearer of

redemption, providing the seeker with a beneficial
karman.

Laying aside greed, hatred, and blindness
through your own efforts grew less important
than the drive, aided by supernatural forces, to find
traces of Buddha's nature—and therefore also of
his insights—within yourself. This prompted the
followers of the Mahayana to a new era of optim-
ism, which resulted in a plethora of writings as
early as the 1st century BC. Some texts were called
*sutra*, others *shastra*—a significant difference,
depending on the author's view of himself.

A sutra is supposed to contain the original
words of the Buddha—teachings that the historic
Master had to hide from his contemporaries who
would not have understood them. Other sutras
are said to be the pronouncements of the
transcendent Buddha whose veracity is therefore
not open to question. A shastra, on the other
hand, is clearly the work of an earthly scholar,
sometimes of someone very famous, who, while
interpreting a sutra, happened upon the Buddha's
true intentions.

*Prajnaparamita* ("wisdom which has gone
beyond") is a concept that was continually the
subject of commentaries and interpretations.
The Mahasanghikas had already replaced the
"knowledge" (*jnana*) of the Old School with
"wisdom" (*prajna*). Knowledge meant deciding
between right and wrong, between yes and no,

Palm leaf manuscript
from Bihar, north India,
made between 1150
and 1175, with a sutra
text. In the center, an
image of the Buddha
entering parinirvana (see
also photos page 169
and page 173).

Prajnaparamita. Back cover of a palm leaf manuscript from the last quarter of the 11th c. At the center, the four-armed female Bodhi-sattva Prajnaparamita ("transcendent wisdom") with worshipers.

and dealt with concepts pertaining to this world. But, for the disciples of Mahayana, knowledge encompassed only a part of reality. Wisdom, on the other hand, was for them something super-rational, something that could not be grasped or fulfilled by the mind, a perfect condition, enabling transcendence to nirvana. This wisdom, slumbering in each and every one of us, could not easily be induced to emerge by any particular method. But through the enactment of rituals, it could become the center of consideration. Thus, a cult arose around prajna-paramita, later personified as a female bodhisattva who helped those who were suffering to attain liberation. For mankind, the task was thus clearly laid out: To recognize the prajna within themselves, to find liberation from the ballast of the mundane, thereby opening up the way to the hereafter. This is the philosophic preamble to the Buddhism of faith that developed later (see page 68).

Another central concept of the Mahayana is *shunyata* ("emptiness"), which refers back to one of the basic insights of the early teachings—that there is no I (as traditionally imagined). The world is empty, it has no substance. The Buddha, who recognized this, wanted to make it clear that we attach our lives to illusions and allow ourselves to be led on their account into false, unhealthy deeds. The concept of "emptiness" at the same time was equated with pain and temporality; it had certain negative connotations to which the Mahayana did not entirely ascribe. On the other hand, the Mahayana made a substantive out of the older

"There is nothing to understand, nothing at all, since there is nothing proclaimed and nothing explained."
    *Astasahasrika Prajnaparamita, second paradox on the Buddha's teach-ings; "nothing" is a synonym for emptiness.*

concept, and this allowed them to view emptiness from a new perspective. Because of this very emptiness, a fundamental sameness of being pervaded subject and object, being and thing, samsara and nirvana. The recognition of the self as emptiness brings with it its own cure: Emptiness is identical to that which cannot be contained in language, to the Absolute.

The question of whether the world filled with emptiness is real or illusory has a fascinating answer that may be a touchstone for contemporary modes of thought. The Fata Morgana, as we know, is an illusion, pursued by the thirsty man until he dies of exhaustion. A false image deceives him and propels him into death. But how can we maintain that other things are real or more real? Ultimately, all judgments are based on impressions made upon the senses—on feeling, tasting, hearing, and smelling—all of which we could call into question with equal validity. Even the empirical criteria would be nothing more than mere illusion to the Mahayana. On the other hand, the Mahayana strives to reserve judgment and to find a medium between the real and the unreal for this reason: A dream is reality as long as one sleeps; reality, a dream as long as one lives.

The Mahayana school that was devoted especially to the prajnaparamita is called *Madhyamika*, the "Middle Doctrine" school of Mahayana Buddhism. Madhyama refers to the middle way between being and nonbeing. If something is said to exist, this thing is thought of as eternal and indestructable. But the Madhyamikas argued that this was just as false as the opposite claim. The truth, formulated by the Buddha as "dependent origination" (see page 34)—that is, emptiness—lies in the middle. For this reason, both corroboration and denial are to be avoided. In emptiness there is no difference between yes and no: Thus, only the one who finds the middle way can attain liberation.

That emptiness is not identical to nothing can be clearly demonstrated through an example. The introduction of the number zero in mathematics (erroneously attributed to the Arabs) in fact came about in ancient India, in close connection with the Mahayana formulation of emptiness. Zero has a special value: It refuses to comply with addition, subtraction, multiplication, or division, but nevertheless is a deciding factor between gain and loss.

Nagarjuna, the great southern Indian teacher of the Mahayana and founder of the New School of Wisdom, protected by serpents. Detail from a modern Nepalese thangka.

This school of thought reached its peak in about 200 AD with the southern Indian philosopher Nagarjuna. The son of a brahman, Nagarjuna had studied in the famous monastery of Nalanda and later became a teacher in Nagarjunikonda and Amaravati. Like so many others, he claimed to be in possession of the Buddha's original words. As the Master set in motion the wheel of teaching with his discourse in Sarnath, he simultaneously left behind a higher teaching in the divine sphere. This was carefully watched over by snakes (*nagas*) in a cave, until Nagarjuna discovered them there in the form of written testimony.

Nagarjuna's New School of Wisdom insisted that all the articles of faith stemming from men are untrue, must be untrue, and prove only our ignorance. He did not explicitly recognize the idea of a Buddha-nature within us. Liberation consisted in recognizing the higher truth, that all things and concepts are empty, that is, neither being nor non-being. Next to this higher truth resided some kind of conventional truth with which we explain the phenomena of our existence, and the existence of the finally equally empty Buddha. Nonetheless, one kind of truth cannot exist without the other, for it is the limited truth of earthly phenomena that first makes possible recognition of the higher truth.

For Nagarjuna, the question "True or false?" is not an expression of opposites per se, but of the viewer's different perspectives. This accounts for the many seemingly paradoxical statements in his work. In order to express the point of view of the

"On this southern side [of the Nalanda monastery] there is a standing representation of the Bodhisattva Avalokitesh-vara. Sometimes he is seen, with a bowl of aromatic essence in his hand, going to the Vihara and walking around it clockwise. South of the statue, there is a stupa built over the hair and nails of the Buddha, which he cut over a period of three months. People who are plagued by serious illnesses and come to walk solemnly around the stupa are usually healed. ... Within the walls there grows an unusual tree, about eight or nine feet high, with a split trunk. Once, while the Tathagata still was on this earth, he threw his tooth pick to the ground at this place, and it started to grow roots. Even though many months and years have passed since then, the tree has neither grown nor shrunk."

*From the report of the Chinese pilgrim
Xuan-zang (7th c.)*

liberated, Nagarjuna could finally only express the unsayable.

In the 5th century, the Madhyamika School split up into two different groups. The Prasangikas believed that Nagarjuna only attempted to prove the others wrong, while the Svatantrikas recognized rules in his teachings that were generally applicable and came—even could only come—from a negating approach. Around 1000, the teachings of the Madhyamikas disappeared from India, but continued to be influential in Tibet and reached even into China, thus being of quite some importance for all of eastern Asia.

In the ruins of the Buddhist monastery university of Nalanda in north Indian Bihar, where Nagarjuna studied, central courts and monks' cells can still clearly be seen. Nalanda was supposedly founded about 440 AD under the Guptas, and housed at times up to 10,000 monks and students. Xuan-zang, the famous Chinese pilgrim (see illustration page 69), studied here for five years during the 7th c.

# Mahayana—The Great Vehicle New Ways to Liberation

Vasubandhu and his elder brother Asanga (see illustration page 81) were sons of a brahman, born in Peshavar, north Pakistan. They distinguished themselves in the 4th c. AD as the main exponents of Yogacara. Asanga especially propagated yoga techniques as a means of approaching the Absolute Spirit. Nepalese block print, schematic depiction.

In addition to the teaching of emptiness and the path of liberation that developed out of it on the one side, and the Buddhism of faith on the other, another Mahayana school should be mentioned. This was the only school that formulated the nature of the world, nirvana, and the Absolute in positive terms; all are "mere spirit" (*citta*). Other teachings elucidated what these were not, what one should not ascribe to them. To define them as "mere spirit" means that nothing objectively exists, everything is imagination. This is reflected in one name for this school of Mahayana, Cittamatra. Another name, Vijnanavada ("teaching of consciousness") refers to the fact that, for the followers of this school, the world first came into being through consciousness of it, and that the suffering therein can only end when consciousness is extinguished. Thus, the teachings of Cittamatra carry an idea of early Buddhism, by which human beings are deceived by illusions, to its extreme.

The literary sources of the Vijnanavada date back to the 1st century AD, but the teaching did not come into full flower until 300 years later. The texts that have survived seem in part very confusing; they may well be less than adequate copies, but because of their confusion and inadequacy, it is not possible to elucidate the most complex system of Vijnanavada in minute detail. At best, we can enumerate the basic tenets of the teaching, which maintains that the Absolute is spirit in pure form. By karman, it is disturbed in its motionlessness and moved to create the fiction of a person. This thought-person imagines the "real," nonexistent world of objects, and at the same time creates new karman, which leads to other imaginings. The world, the one imagining it, and also finally the dreamer of the dream are all therefore nothing but dream. The insight that everything is only spirit liberates us from the eternal dream. However, since there is no individual who can recognize this, this act must take place in the Absolute, which will then cease to imagine persons and objects.

Clearly, we have come a long way from the maxim of early Buddhism, that one ought not to brood over the nature of the cosmos. With the Vijnanavada, asceticism, magic, and trance again became significant on the path to liberation. Since our systems of thought are not suited to approach the Absolute, the followers of Vijnanavada resorted to trance in order to extinguish the world of appearances and to make room for hallucinations. This was considered a step toward the pure spirit. This practice gave rise to a third name for this school: Yogacara ("transformation in yoga"). Yogacara disappeared from India at the turn of the 11th century, although traces of it were left behind in Hinduism. It survived, however, more especially in Tibetan Buddhism (see page 106).

## Mahayana today

Mahayana Buddhism not only offers liberation to all of humankind, but also has mapped out several different paths toward this goal, from simple devotion to a highly philosophical approach or through the active practice of virtues. The Mahayana therefore appeals to completely different people. At its base lies a communal feeling; this is also present in the Hinayana but it is mainly limited there to monastic life. The Mahayana, which defined its positions during the 5th century, gave people a sense of security and a feeling of warmth that helped it spread over large parts of Asia.

# The Compassion of the Bodhisattvas

Buddhist believers, longing for the merciful hand of a bodhisattva. Detail from a 19th c. Tibetan thangka.

While the Buddha lingered under the Bodhi tree after his Awakening, he had to face the temptations of the demon Mara: Should he immediately enter nirvana, or should he first spread his teachings among humankind, to offer others the possibility to follow his path? Out of compassion, he decided to set in motion the wheel of teaching. As soon as the Middle Way was made known, however, there would be no further need of a Master. In this sense, the Buddha's Awakening was a unique event. Whoever followed his path and arrived at the goal would no longer need to decide whether they should renounce nirvana for the good of others. Nonetheless, the monks of the Hinayana were constantly accused of egotism. Their efforts to attain the Awakening seemed selfish and arrogant.

Anyone who has visited a Hinayana monastery can likely confirm that many monks seem unable to deal well with this paradox, which resides in the teachings themselves. On the surface the monks appear calm and cheerful, but they are so intensely involved in pursuing the single goal of their lives that they have little in common with other people. Perhaps fixation on the self in such "isolation" becomes inevitable, and yet that very fixation violates one of the fundamental tenets of the teachings.

The Mahayana, aiming at the liberation of many people, therefore developed a different ideal, that of the bodhisattva. This "Awakened Being" does not teach; instead, he or she gives active assistance to humankind. In order to do this, the bodhisattva must relinquish nirvana—the greatest gift conceivable within a Buddhist system of belief. It marks the highest possible step

Buddhist sources recognize some 200 transcendental bodhisattvas, the most important of whom are associated with their own Buddha-land. Buddha Vairocana goes with the bodhisattva Samanthabhadra, Akshobya with Vajrapani, Ratnasambhava with Ratnapani, Amitabha with Avalokiteshvara, Amoghasiddhi with Vishvapani. Later, Manjushri and Maitreya became important bodhisattvas as well. Since the 6th c., female embodiments— among them the Green Tara protecting from dangers, the White Tara helping for the Awakening, and Prajnaparamita preserving wisdom.

in renouncing self-interest and denotes a greater victory over worldly fetters than the lone arhat could possibly achieve. For this reason, in the Mahayana the desire for nirvana took second place to the effort to become a bodhisattva oneself. Believers were promoted methodically, by a kind of schooling, to become bodhisattvas. The path to the peak remained difficult, marked by steps that, for example, are symbolized in the architecture of the famous Borobudur on Java. In the spiritual ascent, six (according to a later theory, ten) virtues must be perfected: Generosity, self-discipline, patience, strength of will, meditation, and wisdom.

That a person would choose such a path staggers the modern mind. For one thing, it leads to realms beyond life; for another, it necessarily entails great effort and suffering, all for the goal of helping others. The first objection is addressed in the teaching of the three bodies (see page 69f.). A bodhisattva is at first only a person striving for Awakening, but because of their infinite love for fellow human beings, bodhisattvas choose not to follow this path to its end. Only on a higher plane, in an intermediate paradise, which the virtuous person can attain after death, do transcendental bodhisattvas exist. These already-perfected beings have supernatural abilities that they use to mediate between the transcend-ental Buddhas and the temporal world, eliminating the burden of a bad karman. Transcendental Buddhas continue to deny themselves the extinction that is nirvana.

What can account for so strong a love for humankind, a love that induces pain, as the bodhissatva must forego nirvana? According to Mahayana teaching, the explanation resides in the thought that all beings are thought to be one, and therefore the bodhisattva is identical with his or her fellow human beings. Thus, love of others never means self-sacrifice. Moreover, one must take into account the Buddhist concept of suffering. Greed, hate, and blindness lead human beings astray; they seek to satisfy their desires and this seals their fate: They must suffer rebirths. Bodhisattvas, on the other hand, endure suffering, as that is the only way they can liberate others (and thereby themselves) from the fundamental evils.

Vajra Tara, a female embodiment of a salutary force. 11th c. stone sculpture from Sarnath, north India.

# Mahayana—
## The Great Vehicle  Mahayana Today

In the 9th century, the number of Mahayana followers exceeded Hinayana believers in India for the first time. Soon thereafter, however, Buddhism in general lost much of its importance in the country of its origin. Its philosophy and rituals there had become so similar to those of Hinduism that often only minor differences could be discerned, and since Hinduism was the religion with the older roots, it came to predominate. Between the 11th and 13th centuries, the last Buddhist monasteries in Bihar and Bengal were abandoned; this was not, contrary to common supposition, due to Moslem invasion.

Mahayana Buddhism, however, had already spread long before to Tibet and China, and from there over to Korea and Japan. This important development is addressed in two other chapters (see pages 106 and 128). In addition, different forms of the Mahayana are housed in Nepal, Bhutan, and Taiwan. **Nepal**, however, is home to a sort of hybrid form of Buddhism-Hinduism, followed by the majority of the people. In **Bhutan**, there is a lamaistic form of Tantric Buddhism, though this is found more exactly in Tibet. In **Taiwan**, where elements of Confucianism are intermixed with the rituals and superstitions

View of the Somapura Vihara in Paharpur, Bangladesh, 8th c. The main shrine arises from the center of the monastic courtyard with a water reservoir.

of folkloric religion, certain echoes of Buddhism may still be discerned.

Naive paintings in the temple of the city god in Tainan, Taiwan.

**Vietnam** is a rare example of a country where the Mahayana has become a part of the modern political arena. The unified Vietnam, as it exists now, has no historical predecedence. Nam Viet ("Land of the South"), the central territory of the Vietnamese people, was found in the north of the country that exists today. From the 2nd century BC to the 10th century AD, this was a Chinese province, sometimes called Annam. The Chinese cultural influence was great, although the inspiration to establish Buddhist monasteries and temples (from the 2nd century AD) was also due to the influence of India. In about 580 AD, a branch of Chinese Chan Buddhism was established (called Thien; see page 145); another was established later, in about 820 AD. Other Mahayana schools, based on Chinese models, also existed.

When, after many failed attempts, the Vietnamese finally achieved independence from China in 938 AD, it was their turn to nurture expansionist dreams. The Indianized Hindu people of Cham found themselves

Most of the Mahayana texts in Sanskrit still in existence come from Nepal, where the historical Buddha was born. There the tradition of copying palm leaves was rigorously preserved. Since the material survives only a certain number of years, the holy texts had to be copied again and again to preserve them.

**85**

The Wheel of Teaching
on a Vietnamese
assembly hall.

caught between the Khmer and the Vietnamese.
They moved their capital Champa to the south but
were nonetheless completely defeated there in 1471.

Meanwhile, from 1407 to 1428 AD, the north was
again occupied by the Chinese, this time by the
troops of the Ming emperor, who sought to suppress
Buddhism in Vietnam just as he tried to do at home.
Just as in the 12th century when Taoism had gained
hold in the north of Vietnam after the ousting of the
Chinese, this time Vietnam's rulers converted to
Confucianism and began to persecute Buddhists.
In the 16th century, when Vietnam was once again
split in two hostile camps—north and south—Buddhism was again supported. After the union of the
two parts of the country in 1802, Buddhism again
flourished.

The south, which had been a bone of contention
between the Khmer and the Vietnamese for
centuries, remained weak and was an easy catch for
the French in 1857. They named their colony
Cochinchina (later South Vietnam), adding to it the
protectorates Annam and Tongking (North Vietnam)
some time later. The European
influence served to weaken
Buddhism, especially in the south,
where Christian missionaries
directed their proselytizing efforts,
at least toward the upper classes.
A Buddhist reform movement
formed around 1920 and became

Incense burning in a
Vietnamese temple to
call down the mercy of
the bodhisattvas.

an important force against the colonial rulers and for social reforms.

During World War II, a number of the reform-minded Buddhists supported the Japanese occupying forces, while others gave their support in the communist Viet Minh. This rift among the Buddhists was aggrandized through the First Indochina War (1946–1954) with the subsequent division of the country into North and South. Agreement first became possible when Catholicism was propagated in the South under the dictatorship of the Ngo brothers, and the Buddhist monasteries lost their most important financial benefactors. The Buddhists then united to form a third force, besides that of the government on the one side and the union of Viet Minh and South Vietnamese rebels (Viet Cong) on the other side. The position of the Buddhists aggravated the dictators' fears that they could not hold the country, and they therefore turned to the United States for aid. In June 1963, an almost eighty-year-old monk immolated himself, publicizing throughout the world the deplorable state of affairs in South Vietnam. When the Vietnam War (1964–1975, known outside the United States as the Second Indochina War) ended with the victory of the communists over the last bastion of Saigon, a time of reprisals again began for the Buddhists. They had failed to stand decisively on the side of the Left and were moreover feared for of their potential power. It was not until 1987 that the Buddhists were allowed to reopen their monasteries and temples.

Self-immolation of an eighty-year-old Buddhist monk in June 1963 to protest the deplorable situation in South Vietnam.

In addition to the large communities of Mahayana Buddhists in the above-named countries, minorities are also to be found in **Singapore**, **Brunei**, and **Malaysia**. These are mainly Chinese Buddhists, who also wield considerable economic power. In contrast to the Theravada Buddhism on Sri Lanka, there is no country where Mahayana has state support. Since the 15th century, no further prominent places of worship have been built.

### Magical, folkloric foundations

The Buddha prophesied that his teachings would disappear within five hundred years of his death. But by the time Buddhism emerged in its Tantric form, well over half a millennium had passed and the followers of Buddhism were forging new perspectives with unbroken vigor. The first preserved Tantric Buddhist writings date from the 3rd century AD, but, since these reveal an open system, rich in nuances and popular cult elements, it is reasonable to assume that basic texts must have been around for several centuries prior to this time.

Buddhism had become an enormous edifice of philosophies and ritual practices. At its peak stood the body of thought known as the Early Teaching, which remained valid despite extensive reinterpretation. But the tolerance inherent in Buddhism allowed its very foundations to grow to confusingly vast dimensions. Tantrism was a movement that sprang from the roots and spread upward out of popular beliefs and folklore; this popular grounding gave Buddhism a new kind of strength. Western accusations that Tantrism is mere decadence are patently unfair. "Wine and women in the name of religion," became the taunt of certain Puritanical circles in Europe, but such derisive dismissal ignores the historical development of Buddhism and the manifold Tantric practices and schools.

The popular-magical foundations of Buddhist teachings stretch back to the times of Siddhartha Gautama himself. For example, the Buddha's disciple Maudgalyayana (see page 24) was able to attain extraordinary physical and parapsychological abilities (*siddhi*) through spiritual meditation. Later such siddhis were catalogued in detail and were viewed as high goals. The person who could master meditation was believed to be able also to master natural forces; he or she could tame wild animals, arrest epidemics, resurrect the dead, walk on water, change the height and shape of his or her body at

Tibetan Lama wearing a bone apron made of human bones. Vajra, the thunderbolt, is in his right hand; in his left is a sand clock drum, symbol for the reputation of the teachings. Historic, colored photograph, early 20th c.

will, hear and see over great distances, read thoughts, and see into the future. These marvels, however, were not pursued for the sake of self-aggrandizement, but served the highest goal, liberation. Belief in such powers reveals how very high people's expectations of religion and its leading figures were.

In the spirit of the times and in line with the traditions of the country, many people tried to cultivate occult abilities while bypassing the rigors of meditation and self-discipline. Instead, they participated in superstitious rites. It is not always easy, however, to distinguish between these two paths toward supernatural accomplishment; the practice of meditation encompasses certain magical elements: For example, rigorous control of breathing is supposed to give the practitioner control over seemingly involuntary bodily functions (see page 42). Out of such experiences, Indian thinkers formulated mystical means of communicating with the divine.

The parallels between ancient cultures of the West and those of the East may seem obvious in this context, but it is important to bear in mind that these parallels are not necessarily indicative of cross-cultural influence. The congruence of beliefs is probably due in many instances to shared spiritual experiences anchored in popular thinking. The Indian teacher or guru habitually initiated followers

Depiction of two sorcerers and mystics (*mahasiddha*) from the late Indian Buddhist period, striving for liberation by means of Tantric cult practices. Detail of murals from the Manjushri shrine in the Alchi monastery, Ladakh (north India), 11th/12th c.

Amulett (Wheel of Teaching) with inlaid turquoise, a stone very popular in the Himalayas, where it is thought to ward off demons. Tibetan jewelry, mid-20th c.

The magical dagger Phurbu, known as "Demon-nailer" or "Spirit Knife," has in its classic form a three-edged blade made of different metal alloys. The handle is set with the heads of apotropaic protective figures, with fierce expressions. According to Tibetan tradition, the Phurbu can "nail fast" the demonic adversaries of Buddhism.

**Following page:**
One of the world-famous sandstone sculptures of Khajuraho, 10th/11th c., north India. The intimate depictions of lovers and sexual practices are permeated with Tantric philosophies which also influenced contemporaneous Buddhist thought.

by sprinkling water on them—a parallel to the Christian baptism. Here as well as there, incantations were uttered to ward off evil spirits. The religions of India, and Buddhism in particular, evolved more elaborate methods for the recitation of such formulas than was the case in the West. A complicated system of sayings (*mantra*) was supposed to facilitate direct contact with the level of divinity. Ritual dances and hand movements (*mudra*) served a similar purpose.

Out of context, much of this appears to be mere superstition: In context, the aim was to discover the fundamental identity of all existence, to experience the emptiness of both the divine world and that of appearances behind complex rituals and imagery. Gods are not; they are created by humans, just as they are represented by the artist who draws upon traditional texts for physical images. No other world religion has been able to span such an extended bridge between simple popular belief and its theoretical philosophy.

The same is true of the sensual-erotic aspects of Tantrism. In Tantrism, fundamental human needs are linked with much older cults of nature and fertility, and these were again are integrated into the literary traditions of erotic mysticism. The age-old rituals surrounding a mother goddess became in Tantrism part of teaching about the renunciation of worldly things through sexual abstinence. This paradoxical synthesis proved to be a construction that has continued to fascinate people into the present day.

**The Tantra in Hinduism**

There is a simple village in the heart of India, hundreds of miles from the nearest city, that has been equipped with an airport for decades—a curiosity that arose to meet the demands of modern tourism. The name of the village is Khajuraho, and it is known for a cluster of temples that are especially famous for their sculptures. On the walls of the temple, visitors can see *maithunas*, lovers engaged in sexual intercourse, among them whole groups of women and men, absorbed in conventional and unusual sexual practices. The images are surprising, perhaps entertaining, but ultimately puzzling: What, after all, do these figures depicted in sexual activity have to do with the function of a temple?

Most modern Indians apparently share this perplexity: The Tantric form of Hinduism, once quite influential in Khajuraho, was combated first by the Indo-Islamic rulers and later by the British. For this reason, only relatively moderate teachings survived; these are primarily the thoughts and practices of the "Right Hand." Followers of this variant of the Tantra were mainly members of the upper class; its decisive feature was the male principle of the divine, to which human appetites were sublimated.

Tantrism's critics and defenders alike have preferred to focus their

Shiva and Parvati, the divine married couple, and their child Skanda. Lead, pewter, and bronze sculpture from the 12th c. from southern India. Shiva wears his hair in the typical braided crown, both lower hands held in a protective or wish-ful-filling gesture. From his left shoulder to his short hip cloth, the Brahman cord adorns the god. Parvati (also: Uma) wears her hair piled up in a so-called basket crown, has a longer hip cloth and like her divine husband sits comfortably in *lalitasana* (see page 173).

"Intentionally or not, 'life' is continually regenerated through the desire for love. Thus, some cultural communities in the East and West have at times indulged in unadulterated sen-sual desire and in its incitement through female charms, rais-ing this natural drive to an art form through the pure pleasure in naked-ness: To be found on Hindu temples as well as in the rock and pop generations. Antitheses found

attention on the beliefs of the "Left Hand," at the center of which is the feminine principle (*shakti*) of the divine. Shakti is the creative, energizing force of the gods. In sculpture and paintings, Shakti is depicted as wife or companion at the side of the god or in sexual union with him. The most popular divine couple in Tantric Hinduism is Shiva and Parvati. Both gods are often depicted with terrifying features, demonstrating the potential danger of energies so powerful that they can only be ordered and tamed through sexual contact.

What, in fact, is Tantra? The term has several meanings: One is "writings," another is simply "main theme." Most Tantric texts are complicated, sometimes deliberately misleading, and full of extremely distinctive symbolism. They contain a secret knowlege that for many centuries was only passed on orally. The Buddhists engaged with this knowledge maintain that the texts were originally buried by the Buddha's disciples. In any case, beginning in the 5th century, the Tantras took written form. They are not supposed to represent a complete teaching but are, rather, a compilation of various methods by which human beings may approach the divine. Because the Tantras in their system of interpretation are not readily accessible, ordinary readers or novices require a teacher to understand them. After their initiation, initiates meet in circles, in order to pursue Tantric exercises that were vilified by later generations.

The idea of secret knowledge is reminiscent of Vedism and Brahmanism. Here, too, priests functioned as the rigorous keepers of sacrificial formulas and incantations that they passed on to only a few select followers (see page 26). The same method was used with the Tantras, but this time it excluded not the ordinary person but the ruling classes. The underpriviledged, excluded from the Vedas for centuries, created their own teachings based on popular beliefs; they kept them just as secret as any Brahman ever protected Vedic knowledge, and were just as suspicious of outsiders. It is not surprising, then, that Tantric Hinduism totally rejected the caste system and patriarchy and condemned such excesses of the orthodox teachings as the burning of widows. The moral strength of Tantrism has, however, often been ignored by its critics.

On the other hand, certain "Left Hand" Shiva sects actually performed rites that are difficult to justify and from which it is hard to extract any meaning. Sects that worshipped Parvati as the terrifying goddess Durga or Kali sometimes practiced so-called black magic or even human sacrifice. The Aghoris ("Worshipers of the Not Terrible") rigorously opposed many earthly conventions; they refused to wear clothing and ate excrement and human flesh. The Kapalikas performed a ritual in which they drank alcohol out of human skulls. There were also cults in and around grave sites. Characteristic of Hindu-Tantrism is the desire to find the path to liberation through orgiastic acts. At first glance, all of these practices—in which fear and death became objects of fascination—seem diametrically opposed to asceticism and worldly renunciation, but on closer examination, we may make out a deep inner connection between the two seeming polarities, a connection

expression—at times intermittently, at times concurrently—in hypocrisy or prudery or in the realization of the *coincidentia oppositorum*: From love and death, from life and decay and new becoming, from the liberation of sexuality, the foundation for a new union."

*Klaus Fischer,*
Erotic and
Asceticism in the
Cult and Art of India

Human skull, set with bronze and decorated with turquoise, to ward off demons. Tibet, late 19th c. As ritual drinking cups, such *kapala* or skulls were filled with blood, sometimes with wine, in Tibetan Tantric Buddhism.

# Magical Sexual Practices

"The ceremonies culminate in the physical intercourse of those taking part in the initiation rites," wrote a 19th-century European critic about Tantrism. "Each couple represents Bhairava and Bhairavi [Shiva and Devi] and so for an instant becomes one with them. That is *srichakra*, the 'holy circle' or *purnabhiseka*, the 'perfect consecration,' the essential act, or more exactly: The stage prior to liberation, the highest rite of mystic delirium ... But actually, a shakta of the Left Hand is almost always a hypocrite and a superstitious libertarian."

Indian sources often issue the same message.

The holy writings of Brahmanism are filled with abhorrence of the sexual rites or sacrifices common in eastern India. Up until the time of the Mauryan emperors, the Ganges Delta had served as an unbreached barrier to the Aryan invaders. Everything that lay on the far side was considered barbaric; this very fact, however, encouraged speculation. It now seems that Bengal was in those days where peoples fled to escape from the Aryan advance. Their cult had a mother goddess and was absorbed into Brahmanism at a later date. Bengal remained the center of sexual-magical practices and therefore had a decisive influence on the Tantras. In the West, the blood cult surrounding the goddess Kali, encountered by the British colonial rulers in Calcutta, became especially well known.

*Panchatattva* arose from pre-Aryan rites: The participants, sitting in a circle, abandoned themselves to the enjoyment of the five (*pancha*) M's that were stridently rejected by the orthodox: *Madya* (an intoxicating drink), *mamsa* (meat), *matsya* (fish), *mudra* (roasted grains), and *maithuna* (copulation). The ascent to higher spiritual power was sought in wallowing in the forbidden, with

Protective god (*yidam*) Kalachakra in sacred enjoyment of love (*yabyum*) with his consort (*prajna*). Gold-plated bronze from south Tibet, 16th c.

Chinnamasta. Headless form of the goddess Durga (Kali) dancing over a couple in *purushayita* (position in which the woman dominates). Left and right initiation goddesses with skull pendants and blood-filled bowls. Modern Indian miniature.

the aim of overcoming revulsion and killing off lust. The Buddhist counterpart, we should note, consisted of disobeying the five highest rules of the monastic order.

The fact that the number five determined the measure of conduct shows the extent to which rituals were imbued with belief in magic. Up until the (surprisingly early) introduction of the decimal system, Indians counted on the fingers of one hand the five senses, the five elements, the five world regions, and so on. The number five also symbolized the union of heaven and earth. As one among the five M's, therefore, maithuna cannot be considered to occupy a

central position or to constitute the sole aim of Tantrism.

On the other hand, a union—not only in a physical sense—was thought to have a creative force: Life arose from it, as did fruits, including those of knowledge. Ecstasy therefore entailed bliss, and, conversely, bliss entailed ecstasy. In Hindu art, the dissolution of polarities is symbolized most clearly in the physical union of Shiva and his shakti: Shiva, symbol of the extinction of the world, becomes one with the creative, fruitful Parvati. When awakened through the sexual act, the feminine force, present in the body of every human being, allows itself to be used for higher aims.

based on their mutual renunciation of the normality
of existence. Like the more palatable methods of the
"Right Hand," they have no meaning in and of
themselves, but derive their legitimacy from their
goal, which is liberation from the normalcy of the
"false."

### The mystical world view

Eastern India had a decisive influence on both the
Hindu and the Buddhist schools of the Tantra.
Between the 8th and 12th centuries, during the Pala
dynasty, aristocratic benefactors in this region
supported the Buddhist teachings in India one last
time. New monasteries were created while older
institutions, such as the famous university of
Nalanda (see page 79), were expanded to a monumental size. In such institutions lived hundreds of
monks, followers of different schools of Buddhism,
who continually developed new interpretations of the
teachings, thanks largely to the climate that encouraged the animated intellectual exchange of ideas.
Such an atmosphere promoted syncretism, which
constitutes the basic appeal of the Tantras.

In some Indian
representations,
the Buddha appears
as the incarnation
of Vishnu. According
to Hindu belief, the
high god always
embodies himself
in so-called lower
forms. At his ninth
descent, he took
the form of the
Buddha. Herein lies
an attempt to depict
Buddhism as a
mere manifestation
of Hinduism
(Vishnuism).

   In retrospect, it is difficult to specify exactly how
Shivaism (Hinduism) and Buddhism influenced one
another. Still, it is clear that Buddhists saw less
significance in the sexual aspect of the divine than
did the Hindus. Although, for Buddhists, thinking
about the cosmos had been considered unsalutary,
such concerns now moved to center stage. Drawing
on the idea of a cosmic-mythical consciousness,
Buddhists with Tantric predilections had, since the
8th century, concentrated on the liberation of
intuitive energies in order to find traces of the world
order within themselves. Their own sexuality could
serve as a symbol of any kind of union, and so also
for the dissolution of consciousness in emptiness.
This shunyata ("void," see page 76) was then no
longer the crux for philosophical considerations but
assumed mythical status. Followers of the Tantras

therefore attempted to approach this myth through magic powers.

Plainly, things were not as they were commonly assumed to be. Instead, they possessed cosmic references and were embedded in universal structures that could only be made transparent with an understanding of Tantric methods. At this point, metaphysics united with magic. The highest aim of the student—only the initiated could pass the magic-mystical intimate knowledge on to others—was to become a *vajrasattva*, a "diamond being." He then incorporated the qualities of the personified Vajrasattva, the highest Buddha, as well as containing and ruling within himself the complexities of the universe. Vajra, the thunderbolt, reminiscent of the Vedic religion and the most powerful weapon of the Aryans, assumed the qualities of the diamond—hard and pure—symbolizing in turn the teachings and the Awakening. These, however, cannot be learned or experienced, but only grasped spiritually. The Tantric framework is such that, in every thought, in every image, a mystic vision "flashes," mediating between man and the cosmos.

As a symbol of the Absolute, the thunderbolt or Vajra, also known as lightening- or diamond sceptre, became the main symbol of esoteric Buddhism, and represented the male principle, as opposed to the bell representing the female principle. The tool in the photo is of fire-gilded bronze and was poured in Japan during the Fujiwara era (10th–12th c.), modeled on a Chinese original.

## Macrocosmos and microcosmos

The Tantric sense of life grows out of the supposition that everything in the universe is interwoven. The Renaissance premise that man is the measure of all things is utterly alien to Indian thought. Tantric Buddhism postulates Adibuddha as the source of order throughout the universe, actively fostering strength and tranquility in each and every being. He is the only reality behind all the apparent beings and apparent materials. Therefore, the visible world is the manifestation of his existence. Whatever exists here must necessarily have its counterpart beyond the temporal; this clearly distinguishes these concepts from the dualism of Near East salvation religions, such as Christianity.

The Tantric-Buddhist belief in the analogy between microcosmos and macrocosmos explains its followers'

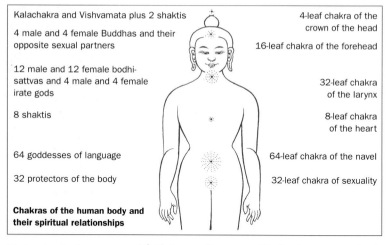

Kalachakra and Vishvamata plus 2 shaktis

4 male and 4 female Buddhas and their opposite sexual partners

12 male and 12 female bodhi-sattvas and 4 male and 4 female irate gods

8 shaktis

64 goddesses of language

32 protectors of the body

4-leaf chakra of the crown of the head

16-leaf chakra of the forehead

32-leaf chakra of the larynx

8-leaf chakra of the heart

64-leaf chakra of the navel

32-leaf chakra of sexuality

**Chakras of the human body and their spiritual relationships**

Tibetan visualization diagram. Contemplation of the sun's disc, the flat disc of the moon and the lotos blossom, in connection with the recitation of suitable and efficacious syllables, should lead the meditator to a Tantric identification with the divine. But even this is only a final illusion and will be overcome by the recognition of the emptiness of all that is imagined.

great faith in occult powers. Meditation, as practiced in the West, is a method for disciplining body and mind. In India, meditation is a means of strengthening the spirit, which is striving to rediscover itself and its real home in higher spheres. Through yoga, the human being ascends to celestial realms; conversely, through cult rituals, he or she can call down the divine into his own soul. The temporal and the eternal, opposites in Western salvation religions, are here harmoniously united.

Tantric texts propose several methods to enable us to perceive the identity between micro- and macro-cosmos. The goal of yoga is to set aside purposeful acts that chain the spirit to the conscious but empty world. Through a progression of exercises, the contact with cosmic centers in the body (*chakra*) grows closer and closer until one finally arrives at a vision of the macrocosmos. Similarly, images of gods—to the Western eye, mere works of art—can be a window into the interconnectedness with the All-One. Conscious breathing (see page 42), as well as the rhythmic recitation of short texts or the repetition of certain sounds, enable communication with the macrocosmos. It is the goal of Tantric Buddhism that, by way of such exercises, the individual human being should come to discover the divine in him- or herself and should learn to control his or her body according to the cosmic mode.

Similarly, the concept of a macro-microcosmic unity has left its imprint on Eastern methods of healing (pressure point massage, acupuncture, etc.) The effectiveness of these methods, which lie outside the mainstream Western devotion to clear cause-and-effect, is based in part on visualizations which are in turn based on cosmic references. Parts of the body correspond to colors, colors to elements, and these again to worlds or gods. So, for example, water is given the color white; the earth is given the color yellow; both are friendly colors, whereas the colors considered evil—red, green, and blue—are assigned to fire and ether (or air). Even syllables form a part of this cosmic system: "MA" is the spine of the world, shown in Mount Meru, which is blue in the east, red in the south, yellow in the west, white in the north, and green in the center. The recitation of syllables therefore has the power to send motion through an entire world until it comes around to affect the individual who uttered the sounds.

This permeation of the macro-microcosmos takes place on all levels and is so complex that only a small handful of people is able to comprehend its laws. And only these can become teachers of the secret

The magical diagram of the ten directions belongs to the numerous Tantric-Buddhist means of orientation and aid, here in a modern mural from a Bhutanese monastery.

"Om. Mani padme. Hum." Mantra of the Avalokiteshvara, here embossed on a prayer wheel. Om and Hum represent the beginning and the end and symbolize totality. Mani padme ("O you jewel in the lotos") stands for the Absolute contained in everything as well as the jewel *cintamani*, which fulfills every wish and which Avalokiteshvara, the master of the six syllables, holds in his hands. Rightly called the prayer most often spoken in the world, its formulation can be traced back to the 1st C. AD.

Tantric knowledge. In such conceptions Buddhism has come full circle: It has returned to the world from which it arose, the world of magical secrets guarded by the Brahmans, the very world from which the Buddha had sought liberation.

### The heaven of the gods in Tantric Buddhism

In Tantric Buddhism, the home of the gods is thoroughly suffused with this rich system of cross-references. The five jinas, the rulers of the Buddha-lands, were mentioned in the previous chapter in connection with the Mahayana. According to the faithful, they were Buddhas right from the start— never people, other-worldly or supra-earthly creatures. Each of them was assigned one of the four cardinal directions according to magic criteria, and therefore there is some slight variance to the Mahayana: Akshobhya ("The Imperturbable") stands for permanence and is master over the center; Vairocana ("The Sun-like") rules in the east; Ratnaketu (in Mahayana, Ratnasambhava—"The One Born in the Precious Jewel") rules the south; Amitabha ("The One of Infinite Light") reigns in the west; and

Akshobya, one of the five transcendent jinas, lord of the eastern Buddha-land enthroned on a lotos. His right hand sinks in the earth-touching gesture (*bhumisparshamudra*; see illus. page 170). Gilded bronze from eastern Tibet or western China, mid-19th c.

Anghavajra (in the Mahayana, Amoghasiddhi—"The Incorruptible") resides in the north. These jinas also represent the five elements, the five human senses, or the five colors, which again correspond to the beginning letters of their names. The symbolism attached to the number five has already been mentioned.

The Adibuddha, the personification of the Absolute, is known to appear in three different forms: First as the already mentioned Vajrasattva with the thunderbolt (*vajra*) symbolizing the masculine attributes and the bell (*ghanta*) symbolizing the

The "sun-like" Vairocana, here four-headed, sits on a lion throne and folds his hands to the "Seal of the Awakened Peak" (*bodhiagrimudra*). Mural from Alchi, Ladakh, 11th/12th c.

feminine. As Vajradhara, the Adibuddha holds his arms crossed so that the male symbol falls on the left, the "female" side of the body, and the female symbol falls on the right, the "male" side. This gesture symbolizes the elimination of polarities in the Absolute, offering a glimpse of the global harmony to which the Tantra continually refers. In the Adibuddha's appearance as Samanthabhadra (in the Mahayana, a bodhisattva), depicted in bodily union with his partner Samantha-bhadri, the idea of universal harmony is yet plainer.

The Adibuddha as Vajrasattva ("diamond-like being"). As embodiment of the Absolute, Vajrasattva holds a vajra or thunderbolt in his hands. Gilded bronze from Nalanda, north India, 13th/14th c.

The transcendent Buddhas were assigned female powers, in addition to heavenly bodhisattvas together with their shaktis, as well as earthly Buddhas. Such a proliferation of Buddhas and bodhisattvas

Ratnasambhava, the
transcendent Buddha of
the South, surrounded
by Mahabodhisattvas.
Nepalese painting based
on an Indian tradition
dating back to the
10th c.

supposedly made the teachings more accessible to
lay believers, who could more readily visualize
complicated concepts when those concepts were
dressed up as gods.

Finally, the gods of Brahmanism as well as a host
of fabled creatures inevitably made their way into the
Tantric Buddhist pantheon. Often they are frightening figures such as the goddess Marichi with a pig's
head or the *dharmapalas*. The terrible power of the
latter was immense, but when they were absorbed
into Tantric Buddhism, they had to obey the Buddha
and were forced to serve as "defenders of the teachings" (*dharmapala*). A step lower in the hierarchy
are the *yidams* (protective gods) and *dakinis* (furies,
see photo page 127), followed by 33 Vedic deities
(see page 8), eight mother goddesses, titans, and

finally good and bad spirits (for example, *yakshas, rakshasas*).

Over the centuries, the gods of Hinduism were also imported into the nether regions of the Tantric-Buddhist pantheon, where they were revered as the personifications of various magical powers. For the spiritual leaders, this panoply simply remained the pictorial expression of deception (*maya*), that deception that early Buddhism had called the world. The majority of the faithful, however, came to think of the gods in the Tantric heaven as a reality. Their cult was modulated more and more to suit the general Indian conceptions and customs, so that at last, for lay believers, Buddhism and Hinduism melted into one.

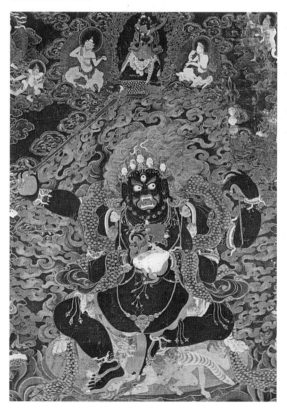

Four-armed Mahakala, one of the Dharmapalas or gods protecting the Buddhist teachings. Such divinities, of frightening appearance and adorned with Tantric attributes, defeat the enemies of Buddhism. Detail from a painting from south Tibet, late 18th c.

Mandala basically means "circle." This circle encloses a diagram comprised up of rectangles, triangles, and other, mainly geometric, shapes that are highlighted with colors or decorated with figures. Enclosed areas, whether abstract or figurative, represent the earthly or heavenly dwellings of the gods. The entire picture is therefore a symbolic representation of the macro-microcosm. Thus, the mandala is an important symbolic instrument (*yantra*) elucidating cosmic connections for those meditating. It can represent an all-encompassing view or it can be limited to parts of the Tantra, such as the nature of a certain god or a particular concept of the teaching. The mandala is always patterned

The blueprint of the Borobudur, erected on Java, Indonesia, between ca. 700 and 915, a pilgrimage shrine with a length of about 330 feet at the base; it rises in four graded terraces and three circular elevations to form a three-dimensional mandala.

according to a more or less uniform structural principle.

A good example is the Vajra-dhatu mandala, which shows the way to salvation. The viewer's thoughts move from the outside into the mandala, from the periphery to the center. First, we meet first three concentric rings: the fiery ring of purgation, the vajra ring of initiation into the teachings, and the lotos ring of purity. When the last ring has been overcome, spiritual rebirth is complete. The believer now finds him or herself in a court that encircles a rectangular palace with four gates each facing toward one of the four cardinal directions. It is important to remember that, in Indian mandalas, east is at the top, while Tibetan mandalas always place the west at the top.

The palace is divided by diagonal lines, producing four triangles. These symbolize the Buddha-lands and have their respective colors. Sukhavati, the kingdom of the Amitabha, for example, can be recognized by the color red. The faithful must now choose one of the Buddha-lands and take the corresponding gate. Here he or she encounters a guard, to whom he must justify his deeds. He will however hardly be denied entry, as the bodhisattva of the chosen land is eager to relieve the faithful of the burden of an evil karman. The way to salvation therefore leads past benevolent bodhisattvas and Buddhas into the center of the mandala, to Adibuddha (see pages 72 and 100), the center of every being. The cosmic vision is now complete, and the faithful has discovered the Absolute within him or herself.

In our description of the Vajradhatu mandala, we mentioned a painting or drawing. The two-dimensional form is of prime importance, appearing on thangkas, the painted scrolls made in Tibet and in the Himalayas (see page 126). A mandala, however, can also serve as the basis of composition for a sculpture or as the blueprint for a temple. The most famous example, and also the largest mandala on earth, is the Borobudur on Java, where the relief and bird's eye views represent the believer's progress toward salvation.

While Westerners may appreciate the aesthetic value of the architecture, sculpture, and paintings based on mandalas, to the Buddhist these are first and foremost aids to meditation. Their artistic merit is secondary to the expression of cosmic interrelations. A kind of peace emanates from the symmetry and centralization of the mandala: The lack of tension is the result of the overarching cosmic vision.

The single dramatic aspect of the mandala lies in the act of its creation: A mandala is formed

Kalachakra mandala, one of the highest Tantric expressions, created under the spiritual leadership of the 14th Dalai Lama (destruction of work see photo on page 44).

during meditation and not while awake. In the meditative ceremony, human intuition is freed from all conscious influences and is thereby transported to a state from which it is able to compress the vision of the cosmos into an earthly symbol. When the work is complete, as far as the meditating creator is concerned, its effect is finished and it is then often destroyed (see page 44). If it is preserved, it becomes a yantra for the meditating observer. His inward sight sees the man-made, cosmic object, until space and time dissolve and a condition of unconsciousness sets in. In this state, the meditating believer experiences the identity of rich variety (the figures on the mandala) and emptiness (content of the mandala) and thereby overcomes all the contradictions of the world of appearances.

### Conflict with Bön

Today in the West, what is considered authentic Buddhism is usually not what has been derived from the original teachings of the Buddha in India, but later forms of the Buddhist religion that has been subjected to many revisions. For many, the Tibetan Dalai Lama, who for many is the quintessence of Buddhism. Though this is fundamentally a misconception, it has been fueled by a number of political factors, including the Chinese occupation of Tibet in 1950, the exile of the 14th Dalai Lama to India in 1959, and the People's Republic of China's incorporation of Tibet in 1965 as an "autonomous" province. In the chilly atmosphere of the Cold War, the Dalai Lama, as a peaceful—and, for the West, useful—opponent of communism, became a "political" concern. The

Dalai Lama's spiritual and personal charisma, magnified by the media, has earned him sympathy around the world.

Tibetan legend describes the creation of the Tibetan people as the union of a monkey with a mountain demon. Although there are reports of a Buddhist text being shown to one early Tibetan ruler in the 2nd century AD, Buddhism first became an important factor in Tibet when the country began to expand politically. Under the 7th-century king, Srong-bstan-sgam-po, pronounced and also known as Songtsen Gampo (he held the title of *dharmaraja*, "religious ruler") and under his successors in the 8th and 9th centuries, Trisong Detsen and Tri Rapaltschen, Tibet expanded as far as Turkestan and China. Over the same span of time, the Tibetans were developing their own form of writing for the Tibetan language; without the means to transcribe their language, translations of Indian-Buddhist writings would not have been possible.

King Songtsen Gampo (left) and King Trisong Detsen (right) in a schematic depiction. Modern Tibetan blockprint on rice paper.

As Buddhism grew in Tibet, its followers ran up against the widespread ancient religion known as the Bön. Bön was characterized by animism and shamanism; its practice sought to influence both natural and human events with astrology, sorcery, spells and rituals, amulets and spirit traps, and through blood sacrifice. But, as Buddhist doctrine spread and gained acceptance, the more amorphous and disjointed Bön, a patchwork of myriad local traditions, began to impose more structure on its own practices, adding to its own teachings to the point where it became, in essence, an entirely different religion after the 8th century than it was before. Following the Buddhist model, the tenets of Bönism were gathered into "vehicles" by its priests, particularly by one Shenrab Miro, whose persona was at the heart of many Bön myths. These texts included rituals pertaining to death, oracular interpretation, and exorcism, among others. The ostensibly new Bön

Shenrab Miro, the great teacher of Bön, appears as a figure of light in a Chorten, the Tibetan form of the stupa. Detail from a Tibetan thangka, early 20th c.

pantheon showed a great debt to the Buddhist Mahayana and Tantrayana traditions. In the 9th century, the Tibetan King Langdarma even managed for a short period of time to promote acceptance of the reformed, more systematized Bön at the expense of Buddhism. The Bön king, however, was murdered, reportedly by a Buddhist monk, in 842 AD.

It is telling, and probably no coincidence, that Buddhism first gained widespread acceptance with the people of Tibet, so long steeped in the practices of Bön, only when Buddhism itself had entered a magic-mystical stage. To be precise, it was the Vajrayana ("The Diamond Vehicle"), that arose in the 4th and 5th centuries AD, that took hold in Tibet. Vasubandhu and Asanga, two brothers from Peshavar (today in northern Pakistan), are believed to have been res-

Bön priest with a wizard's hat, as worshiper of the Shenrab Miro. Detail from the same thangka.

"In the Vajrayana Buddhism becomes a Gnostic religion, one in which neither the intellect nor ethically correct conduct can lead to ultimate knowledge. Instead, the highest goal is esoteric wisdom which, like an ecstatic, enraptured consciousness, can only be reached through complicated rituals. In these rites, as emotions are laid bare, step by step, higher spiritual forms of existence are attained. The boundless compassion of the bodhisattvas is no longer necessary for liberation; what is needed is a teacher who accompanies the novice on the path of awakening and brings him safely to the goal."
*Alexandra Lavizzari-Raeuber*

ponsible for preparing the way for the spread of the Vajrayana, one of the four main streams of the Mahayana, with their Yogacara teaching (see page 81).

The vajra, or thunderbolt, of the Hindu thunderstorm god Indra, symbolized on the one hand the diamond hardness and simultaneous diamond clarity of the Buddhist teachings, and, on the other hand, the impenetrable and indestructable Emptiness (*shunyata*) pervading all material things, the human individual and the world of the gods. An objective existence is therefore just as impossible as the earthly suffering from which the Hinayana sought to liberate humankind. Rather, the aim of believers was to attain an omniscient consciousness ("Clear Light") and a "Pure Illusory Body." Only the Awakened can clearly see the profound unity of Emptiness and Appearance. Thus is the role of the later lamas, the spiritual teachers and monks of Tibetan Buddhism, already set forth (see below). They gave their name to this branch of Buddhism, Lamaism, however, is an epithet that often used disparagingly, as if to indicate a less pure form of the religion.

### The "First Propagation of the Teaching"

The exact date of the first contact between Buddhism and Tibet is a matter of debate. But it is absolutely certain that Padmasambhava ("the lotos-born"), a Tantric Buddhist from the Svat valley (in what is today Pakistan) and an enigmatic sorcerer, carried the teachings of the Vajrayana into Tibet with so much conviction and personal charisma that they have retained their dominance there to the present day. According to legend, Padmasambhava's mission was a continual struggle against demons trying to subvert his efforts, until they were at last subjugated and forced to swear to serve Buddhism ever after. In Tibetan Buddhist iconography, these demons take the form of terrifying figures, though the images often create confusion among Western observers who find it difficult to keep in mind that these fearful figures are not in fact enemies but friends won over to the cause. It is probably more accurate to see in them the assimilated local gods and spirits of Bön, and, at the same time, an expression of the Tantric principle of balancing good and evil, compassion and anger. Under Padmasambhava, the first seven Tibetan monks were ordained in 779 AD; then, in 791 AD, a Buddhist monk was given a more prestigious seat relative to the king's throne than the secular advisors—presaging the later Tibetan "State of God," the Buddhist hierarchy.

Padmasambhava was probably responsible for the construction of Samye, the earliest native Buddhist monastery, at the Tsangpo river (36 miles southeast of the Tibetan capital of Lhasa) in 775. This period in Tibetan history is known as the "First Propagation of the Teaching." An event from this period that is worth noting is the so-called Great Debate, convened at the monastery in Samye in 792. The debate lasted two years, and is supposed to have resolved royal favor toward the Indian Mahayana/ Vajrayana branch of Buddhism over the Chinese Buddhists of the Chan, or Meditation, School. In any case, since then, any ideas resembling Chan (see page 145), in their suggestions that it is possible to attain spontaneous awakening and liberation, have been frowned upon as "Chinese."

Padmasambhava, the lotos-born, became the "Apostle of Buddhism" to the Himalayan countries during the 8th c., achieving his acceptance over folk cults and magical practices. Detail from a Tibetan thangka.

In the mid-9th century, Tibetan imperial ambitions, which had sent troops as far as Samarkand and

Atisha, originally from Bengal, was one of the most important purveyors of Indian-Tantric thought during the 11th c. Contemporary blockprint.

Burma, failed, and with them fell the ruling house. The last representatives of the ruling dynasty moved to the western edge of their former kingdom, to Ladakh, Guge, and Purang. Great Tibet broke apart into a number of petty princedoms. Under such conditions, Buddhism could no longer sustain its position as the "national religion" in central Tibet; it survived the political crisis, however, in a somewhat disguised form that allowed ancient magic folk traditions to reemerge.

## The "Second Propagation of the Teaching"

The truth is not really certain, but this is the picture drawn at the beginning of the 11th century by the learned monk Rinchen Sangpo, whose life marked the beginning of the "Second Propagation of the Teaching." The Buddhist King Yeshesod, who ruled over the small west Tibetan kingdom of Guge, had sent a number of young men to Kashmir to study Buddhism in its highest philosophical form and then bring it back to Tibet. Among those sent by the king was Rinchen Sangpo (958–1055), who stayed in Kashmir for 17 years. After his return, he distinguished himself as a translater (*lotsava*) of Indian writings, reinstated the old monastic rules, and even founded monasteries. The monastery Lamayuru in Ladakh, for example, was supposedly constructed around older buildings under the direction of Rinchen Sangpo.

Marpa, one of the great Tibetan translators. Detail from a Tibetan thangka.

The second great reformer of Tibetan Buddhism was the Bengali monk Atisha (982–1054), whose most important written work is *Light on the Path to Awakening*. At the invitation of the royal house, Atisha traveled to Tibet in 1039 and introduced numerous Tantric teachings into monastic life. From the perspective of religious history,

Atisha was a syncretist, combining the doctrine of an all-pervading Emptiness with the teaching pertaining to the creation of the awakening spirit (see page 120). His syncretistic teaching earned him a broad following; his most important follower was the 11th-century Tibetan Drom Tönpa who founded the Kadampa, or "Bound by Command School," introducing reform into monastic life. At the same time, another Tibetan Buddhist named Marpa (1012–1096) spent 16 years studying with the famous Vajrayana wise man Naropa in Bihar, India. Marpa brought back to Tibet many complex Tantric teachings and techniques. When Marpa returned to Tibet, he lived as a farmer, a married layman, not as an ordained monk, although monks continued to consult him.

Milarepa, ascetic and pupil of Marpa, lived as a hermit in the Himalayas for many years, developing magical abilities. His right hand held to his ear is a gesture typical for his iconography, signifying that Milarepa is listening to the message of the spheres. Detail from a Tibetan thangka.

Marpa's most famous pupil was the enigmatic and reclusive Milarepa (1052–1135), an ascetic who for many years sought the solitude of the mountains before taking on pupils, among them Gampopa (see below), and passing his wisdom on to them in songs. According to the testimony of his contemporaries, Milarepa defied even the icy cold of the Himalayas in winter. Clothed only in a thin white cotton robe, he reportedly used one of Naropa's six meditational techniques to produce his own "internal heat" and thereby survived the extreme temperatures. Naropa's doctrines, we should note, are related to the last and most complex of the Tantric systems: the Kalachakrayana, which is said to have been formulated in the mythic land of Shambhala and to have reached Tibet in 1027 AD.

Under the influence of all these teachings, teachers, and role models, Tibetan Buddhism developed its own particular form. More precisely, various large schools or orders grew up between the 11th and 13th centuries, all built on a common foundation. Each maintained its own version of the teachings and had its own religious hierarchy, as well as independent monastic rules and yoga techniques. This decentralization was due in part to the absence of any central political power in Tibet that could have exerted a unifying pressure on the monasteries. Furthermore, even the Indian tradition, which had been an inspiration and regulatory force for Tibet until then, broke down shortly before the Moslem invasions. After 1200, the great Buddhist universities of India, such as Vikramashila and Nalanda, where Naropa had taught, closed their gates (see page 84).

Tibetan monks sitting above volumes of holy writings. Detail from a Tibetan mural in a Sakya-pa monastery, 18th c.

### Lamaism and the Tibetan "State of God"

Today, if you visit a Buddhist monastery in Tibet or its surroundings (Ladakh, Zanskar, northern Nepal, Bhutan, Sikkim), regardless of the order to which it belongs, you will find many bound written and/or printed pages, stacked methodically on shelves, organized and wrapped in silk: This is where the fundamental tenets of the large orders are set forth. This is the canonic Kangyur, consisting of 108 volumes spanning the Hinayana texts, the prolific Mahayana literature, and the Tantric teachings, rituals, and yoga practices. These stacks of pages are the fruit of centuries of Tibetan diligence in translation. In the 14th century, the Kangyur became the codified basis of monastic life.

Another monumental body of work you may find on the shelves of the Tibetan monasteries is the Tangyur, though it is not generally considered obligatory, as the Kangyur is. In the 224 volumes of the Tangyur are a wide variety of hymns to Buddha, collections of prayers, legends, and texts pertaining to secular knowledge (medicine, grammar, poetry, logic, geneology, time calculations). It also contains commentaries on the Tantras whose various details have been found objectionable by one or another of the different orders. Here the spiritual unity of Tibet ends, and the particular traditions of the monastic orders begin.

Nyingma monk in Gangtok, Sikkim.

Historically, the oldest tradition is the Nyingma-pa ("School of the Elders"—the "elders" in this case refers to the old Tantras), also known as the "Red Hat" or "Unreformed" School. This is the only tradition based firmly on the Tantric master Padmasambhava, who is seen as a second historical Buddha by the members of the order and its followers. Padmasambhava's final esoteric teachings are said to be stored in secret caches (caves, statues, and underground storage areas), from which, at the appointed time, predestined believers known as *tertön* ("revealers of the treasure") will be given the *terma* (variously translated as "treasure" or "revelation"); these scriptures are texts or images that are the key to liberation for the period when they

Frightening figures, here goddesses with animal heads, as they appear to the deceased before rebirth (see page 114). Detail from a Tibetan thangka, 19th c.

Two abbots of the Gelug-pa, the order of the "Yellow Caps." Detail from a Tibetan thangka.

Grain storage area in the south Tibetan monastery Sakya, built in the 11th c., and parent house of the order of the same name.

happen to be found. Probably the most famous term is *The Tibetan Book of the Dead* (*Bardo Thödöl*), read at the bed of the dying, to teach him or her about the intermediate kingdom (*bardo*) between death and rebirth (see page 118). The Nyingma tradition differs from the three other Tibetan Buddhist movements not only in its ostensibly direct relation to the First Propagation of the Teaching, but also in its rejection of central leadership and of a rigid monastery hierarchy. In Nyingma-pa, both are replaced by the meditative experience. In its mostly small, dispersed monasteries (most are found in eastern Tibet), the monks' world view is organized into nine "vehicles" dedicated, in ascending groups of three, to the "radiant body," the "body of complete joy," and the "awakened" or "true body."

The Kargyut-pa also looks back with pride at an unbroken tradition. The name of this order essentially means "Followers of the Transmitted Command" and is today a generic term encompassing several different branches of tradition, of which the karma movement is surely the most influential. According to the order, its "transmitted teachings" may be traced back to the Buddha Vajradhara who communicated his instructions to the great sorcerer Master Tilopa (988–1069). Tilopa in turn transmitted them to Naropa, who disclosed his knowledge to the Tibetan Marpa, and he to

his ascetic pupil Milarepa. It was then under Milarepa's pupil Gampopa (1079–1153) that the order was founded.

The Sakya-pa trace their origin to the famous translater Dogmi (992–1072), who, like Marpa, was initiated into Buddhism in India and studied there. The monastery Sakya in southern Tibet, from which the order takes its name, lies on an old trade route that linked Tibet with the Katmandu valley. When the Mongolians of the Yüan dynasty annexed Tibet during the 13th century, they appointed in succession two noble Sakya grand lamas, Sakya Pandita and Phagpa, to wield administrative power in Tibet. Thus was Tibet ruled for the first time, if only briefly, by priest-kings.

The Kahdam-pa, the order of the "Oral Instruction," was founded by the great translater Drom-tön, who developed important meditation techniques for the purification of the spirit based on the teachings of Atisha. Kahdam-pa has not survived as an independent school,

Mounted Gelug Lama in wintery Tibet.

although its teachings and scripts found their way into other orders, especially into the tradition of the Gelug-pa ("School of the Virtuous"), founded in the 14th century through the efforts of the east Tibetan reformer Tsongkhapa (1357–1419). The members of Tsongkhapa's order could be distinguished by their orange-yellow caps—hence, the nickname "Yellow Hats"—from the habit of the older orders with their red caps. The yellow hats came to symbolize the new religious wave of reform in Tibet. The Gelug-pa turned away from all strongly ecstatic or erotic magical practices and banned the consumption of intoxicating drinks. Emphasis was and continues to be placed on the systematic study of Buddhist writings (especially the non-Tantric philosophy of the Mahayana) and observation of the monastic

Mongolian ruler subdues the Chinese tiger with the help of the chain of the Tibetan Buddhist religion. The political motif belongs to the standard repertoire of wall and scroll paintings in Tibetan monasteries. Here a modern schematic drawing.

13th Dalai Lama (1876–1933) at age 24. Colored historical photograph.

rule. The order became very popular; its membership grew so quickly that many large monasteries and centers for teaching sprang up in rapid succession, including the monasteries at Ganden (1409), Drepung (1416), and Tashilünpo (1447).

By means of its strict monastic hierarchy and centralization, the Gelug-pa became an important element in government in the secular world, especially when, during the 15th century, the power of the Tibetan state began to crumble. The "Yellow Hat" abbot of Drepung, Sönam Gyatso (1543–1588), found a strong political patron in the Mongolian ruler Altan Khan. The ruler conferred upon the abbot the title Dalai Lama (literally, "Great Ocean," suggesting wisdom as wide and deep as the ocean). The abbot, who saw himself as part of a chain of rebirths, bestowed this title on two of his successors, thereby launching a tradition that, in 1617, led to the naming of a child Lobsang Gyatso (1617–1682) from a Buddhist family in central Tibet as the 5th Dalai

Lama. With this "Great Fifth," as he is known in the Gelug tradition, religion assumed political authority in Tibet. Under the protection of the Mongolians, who had converted to the Tibetan version of Tantric Buddhism, arose a theocracy for which the Dalai Lama was the secular authority and, in the person of Panchen Rinpoche ("Great, Precious Teacher," also called Panchen Lama), was also the highest authority in matters of faith. When one of the two leaders dies, a complicated ritual begins: Omens and oracles are consulted to help locate a newborn boy who is believed to be the reincarnation (*tulku*) of the deceased leader. This happened last in 1937 when a two-year-old in the east Tibetan province of Amdo was named the successor of the 13th Dalai Lama, who had died in 1933. In 1940 he was enthroned as the 14th Dalai Lama, and at age 16, he was named head of state. After his flight from Communist-controlled Tibet in 1959, he took up residence in the northern Indian mountainous city Dharamsala. In many political initiatives, faithful to the principle of nonviolence, the Dalai Lama has proven himself a pious and modest champion of the Tibetan people.

Tibetan beggar. Drawing by Sven Hedin, beginning of 20th c.

The admirable composure of the 14th Dalai Lama in the face of the political turbulence in Tibet has won him great sympathy and in some ways produced a tendency to idealize the theocracy. The 9th, 10th, 11th, and 12th Dalai Lamas, however, were all murdered after a short "time in office"—not only because this was advantageous for the Chinese rulers of the Manju dynasty then in power, but also because internal Tibetan religious cliques fought for dominance. It is also by no means purely Chinese Communist propaganda that describes Tibet as an extremely backward country in 1950: It lacked roads and bridges, minimal standards of hygiene, hospitals, secular educational institutions, and contact with foreign countries. Instead, Tibet suffered widespread poverty, high infant and child mortality, and illiteracy. During the centuries when Buddhism

The **wheel of life** (*bhavachakra*), also called the "wheel of existence" or the "wheel of becoming," is a didactic image of the cycle of rebirths. It is often found painted onto the outer wall of Tibetan temples, directly adjoining the entrance. It is also a popular motif in thangkas and block prints. The iconographic origins reach back at least as far as the Ajanta, a series of rock-cut caves with Buddhist frescoes dating back to the 6th century AD, though legend ascribes the iconography to the Buddha himself. When Gautama Buddha's pupil, the magician Maudgalyayana, returned from one of his meditative journeys to the underworld, the Master enjoined him to depict his experiences of the hereafter on a rotating drum.

At the hub of the wheel of life are the "three basic poisons," the forces propelling the cycle of rebirths: passion, hatred, and delusion, symbolized by the red cock, the green snake, and the black pig. Around the center is a sequence depicting the path ascending to liberation and the path descending to the lowest forms of rebirth. The greater part of the wheel of life is divided through its spokes into six areas, denoted by six different colors. They define the six world regions (*gati*) to which rebirths can lead the living: the world of the gods, or heaven world (white), the world of the benevolent gods and demigods known as Asura (green), the human world (yellow), the animal world (blue), the world of the hunger spirits, like a purgatory (red), and the world of hells (black). Often a compassionate Buddha Avalokiteshvara is placed in each of these worlds, pointing to the possibility of exit for the being caught there. The outermost ring of the wheel depicts the Buddhist teaching of the twelve nidanas, the links in the cycle of "dependent origination" (see page 34).

Outside the wheel of existence, free from all rebirths, are the Buddha Gautama, above on the right, and the compassionate Buddha Avalokiteshvara, above on the left (see photo page 125). The wheel itself is held by a demon, lord of death and of illusion, symbolizing the miseries and limitations of existence.

The **Tibetan Book of the Dead** (*Bardo Thödöl*), known since the 15th century, is regarded among Tibetan Buddhists as one of the "treasures" of knowledge left behind by the Tantric monk Padmasambhava (see page 108). Read at the deathbed, it teaches the dying about the intermediate kingdom (*bardo*) that the dead person enters before being reborn into one of the six worlds of the wheel of life. "Thödöl" essentially means "awakening through hearing" and signifies a Tantric way to nirvana, accepted only by Tibetan Buddhists. When the deceased, during a 14-day period of the "terrors of death," has reviewed his or her life with the inner eye in order to recall to the conscious mind the merits and mis-

Thangka on the *Book of the Dead*. Nepal, 19th c. The white Buddha Vajrasattva reveals the visionary gods of the *Tibetan Book of the Dead* to believers. The 42 peaceful ones are in a lower circle, the 58 angry divinities in an upper circle. Only those who, in the intermediate realm, recognize that these supra-human beings are mere emanations of Emptiness, can break out of the cycle of rebirths.

deeds of his karman, after his "external breath" comes to an end, like the falling away of the external, illusory world, he or she experiences a gleaming light that is the ultimate truth. If the person can identify with this truth, then he or she has liberated him or herself for all times and will be "extinguished" and attain nirvana. If he or she cannot perceive the truth in the light, a new conscious body arises and continually encounters new projections and phenomena of light in the world of highest reality, which, though, is not nirvana. The possibility of liberation still exists if the peaceful and frightening images can be recognized as deceptions, as the expression of a clouded or marred karman, resulting from the previous existence. Only after 17 days does the conscious body of the deceased enter into the bardo of becoming, where it is led 31 days later to rebirth.

held secular power in Tibet, the religious traditions had showed themselves basically indifferent to civilization. In an atmosphere of conservative self-satisfaction, Tibetan Buddhism was equally oblivious to its own spiritual development. The lively dispute that had been carried on between the orders for centuries came to a halt under the secular rule of the Gelug, stagnating in the memorization and repetition of traditions.

### Spiritual foundations and techniques

Like other Mahayana movements, the Vajrayana had formulated teachings in which nirvana, samsara, and the self were all equally equated with Emptiness. Unlike "classic" Mahayana, however, the Vajrayana taught that the path to liberation could be abbreviated to the span of a single life. Instead of having to accumulate the merits of karma over many existences, one could attempt direct (within one human lifetime) entry into the highest awakening.

The precursors of the Vajrayana based their teachings in part on those of the southern Indian Mahayana holy man Nagarjuna (around 200 AD), who in his Madhyamika philosophy ("Teaching of the Middle Way") had proclaimed the Emptiness or Non-Being of all things and concepts (see page 77). This tenet became united with the Cittamatra teachings (see page 80), according

14th Dalai Lama (left) as master of a Kalachakra ritual, here banning obstructive beings.

to which the world and its innumerable appearances were merely projections of the conscious mind. The seed of the Buddha-nature, dormant within each living being, makes it possible for people, through meditative exercises in ascending stages, to become aware of the true, monistic, nondualistic nature of Being, that is, Being beyond all the seemingly polarized phenomena and attempts at conceptual categorization. The selfless "spirit of awakening" thereby attained is—according to the Tantrayana—an altruistic spirit, striving for the happiness—the awakening and liberation—of all living beings.

The ascent to the awakening and extinction of the self is a path that consists of exercises in four tantric classes. First, the novice must practice external acts; this stage is known as *Kriyatantra*. In the second stage, *Caryatantra*, he or she combines these external actions with internal processes. In the third stage, *Yogatantra*, the internal exercises become dominant. The last and highest stage is *Annutarayogatantra*; to this class belong the *Kalachakra Tantra*, which are particularly demanding spiritual exercises, laden as they are with the approaching liberation.

Ritual music accompanies sacred acts or ceremonies in Lamaistic monasteries. Here a Bhutanese novice beating the drum.

In the ritual exercises of Tibetan Buddhism, these stages are interconnected, as in the creation of a mandala (see page 104). First, the necessary external actions are performed, like the cleaning of the ground for the mandala, or taking its measure, stepping around it repeatedly. Certain phases of the ritual preparations may be accompanied by cult music. The Vajra master then joins together the external and internal acts by summoning the divinity to be called down within himself (God-Yoga). By chanting *mantras*, holy or "seed syllables," the master visualizes the divine Being in an external picture, which, once finished, is again dissolved in Emptiness.

It is important to remember that the the Vajrayana concept of god has nothing in common with Middle Eastern and Western monotheism or, for that matter, with Hindu polytheism. The gods, with their assigned

Tibetan prayer wheels contain mantras, mystical "efficacious syllables," on strips of paper which begin to vibrate through the turning motion of the metal container, allowing their secret power to unfold. Believers attribute to them a power equal to that of reciting or murmuring mystically potent prayers and syllables.

colors and attributes, are projections of the conscious mind, powers to aid the spirit, and, like all human beings, they too are deceptive images of the final Emptiness. At the same time, they are representatives of beneficial virtues, such as compassion or wisdom, which the meditating person, the creator of the mandala, would like to reproduce within him or herself.

The last and highest class of the Tantras, the Annutarayogatantra, is divided into two levels: a stage of generation, in which the "pure illusory body" of the Buddha arises, as the the five common "marred" elements of living beings—corporality, feelings, perceptions, mental impulses and conscious activity—are purified into those of a Buddha. The second level is the stage of resolution, leading to the "Clear Light." The union of this paramount state of consciousness with the Buddha-body leads to the Vajradhara or Samanthasabhadra condition in which the Absolute (personified as Adibuddha; see page 100) manifests itself, and all contradictions and differences are simultaneously dissolved in the final Unity.

The path to liberation, thus, in Tibetan Buddhism, in contrast with that of classic Mahayana, is a short one; liberation may be attained not through the multiple existences that must disintegrate all the dregs and clouding of the karma, but in a single span of life, albeit one spent in rigorous and unrelenting discipline. Here, then, resides a profound connection with Zen and its concept of a (prepared for) spontaneous awakening (*satori*). Here also lies the reason why, in the 20th century in the West, the "me generation" in its quest for self-realization has found both these late Buddhistic movements so appealing. The paradox of their adoption of these Eastern streams becomes obvious when we compare Western conceptions of self-realization and the Eastern concept of the obliteration of a self that is mere illusion. Nevertheless, Western disciples continue to be fascinated by Eastern spirituality, ready and willing to see themselves as its

## The significance of the lama

While Tantric-Tibetan Buddhism offers what appears to be a short-cut to liberation that somehow abbreviates the cycle of rebirths, it also describes a path that is, because of this very brevity, particularly complex and demanding. As with so many short-cuts, one may only enter this path with especially accurate knowledge of the way and with meticulous discipline. The Tantras are in no respect a precise spiritual travel guide; the follower needs a teacher to initiate and lead him or her onward on the path of liberation. In Tibet, this is the role assigned to the lama. "Lama" is the Tibetan equivalent of the Sanskrit word "guru." It means basically "the higher standing one, the eminent." The title refers to highly qualified religious leaders, not to every Buddhist monk (although the term lama also serves as a polite form of address for Tibetan monks in general). In one of its papers, the Tibetan Department for Religion and Culture, the office of the Dalai Lama in Dharamsala, elucidates the qualities that distinguish a lama: "He must obey his vows and ethical rules, he must

A lama in charge of novices introduces them to the sacred teachings in a Gelug-pa monastery in Lhasa.

a lama: "He must obey his vows and ethical rules, he must possess powers of concentration and discriminating wisdom. He must have greater learning and higher spiritual experiences than his pupils, and must endeavor to attain the highest goal for himself and for others. He must have thorough knowledge of the 'Three Baskets of the Teachings' and must understand the true nature of phenomena. Moreover, he should be skilled in teaching his students and have a great liking and sympathy for them, as well as for all other living beings. He may not let himself be daunted by the difficulties he encounters in the actions he undertakes for the well-being of his pupils." In short, a lama must be thoroughly suffused with the spirit of Buddhist teachings and must be well advanced on the path of salvation. Traditionally, a lama has been

Masked ritual dancers represent dharmapalas, protective patrons of Tibetan Buddhism (compare illustration page 103).

ordained for at least ten years; moreover, he has spent three years as a recluse and has been initiated into the highest and most secret ceremonies by another lama. He is a master of the Tantras, initiates disciples into the mystical world vision, and protects people in general by officiating at specific rituals (such as lama dances). The lama, like the bodhisattva, has seen through the material of reality and could pass away into nirvana, but stays on through compassion as the personification of liberation on earth, a mirror of the Absolute for his pupils. In his Tantric and meditative exercises, the disciple centers his concentration completely on the lama as his spiritual master and maintains continual connection with him, even when the master is not physically present.

The Mahayana world view, with its bodhisattvas (see page 82) mediating between the Absolute and the human world, is evident in Tibetan Buddhism. Thus, the Tibetan concept of tulku, of the reborn lama, whose significance was discussed above, also comes into focus. The eminent teacher, through the strength of his Buddha nature, takes on a human form in a new, as it were, unrefined or loosely knit "body of appearance," in order to continue his work of liberation even after his biological death. The Dalai Lama, the "Ocean-wise teacher," thus, is also known in Tibet as *kundun* ("the one who is present"), as the concrete earthly presence of a bodhisattva. In the case of the present Dalai Lama, we see Avalokiteshvara, the bodhisattva of compassion and the patron saint of Tibet, at work in what is now his fourteenth rebirth. An old prophesy, however, which the Dalai Lama himself

Avalokiteshvara ("the one looking down compassionately") is the most effective Mahayana bodhisattva. He helps humans, gods, animals, and beings of the nether regions. Personifying all-encompassing compassion, he is depicted with 11 heads: His head split at the sight of earthly suffering, Amitabha (see page 73) made 9 new peaceful heads, topped by a tenth angry one to ward off demons, and crowned by Amitabha's own head. Gilded bronze, Sikkim, 19th c.

Tibetan lay artists painting a thangka in Dharamsala, north India.

Thangkas, which are still produced in Tibet and in the Himalayas, are a form of Buddhist art that has become quite popular in the West. These paintings may take the form either of representations of mandalas (see page 104) or of single figures or groups, often compositionally arranged like a mandala. The portable picture scrolls are easily carried on pilgrimages and spread out for devotion. Their main function, however, is to decorate monastic halls, sometimes alongside murals and other paintings, but more often in place of them. The preference for brilliant colors may be explained in part by the darkness of the rooms in which they are hung. Certainly, the vivid colors allow the thangkas to be seen in the relative dimness. But the colors in which the thangkas are painted also correspond to the clear

light of Tibet and to Buddhist color symbolism. The pigments used to make the paints were originally prepared solely from mineral (cinnabar, minium, arsenic sulfide, copper carbonate) or plant (indigo, varnish resin, charcoal, glue) matter. The production process was extremely complicated, especially for the preferred gold tones, and the technical expertise that was required was protected as a secret by the artists. For this reason, the paints were very expensive. They were also water soluble, and thus impermanent. Eventually the original processes were replaced by synthetic products that were also very luminous. Today, thangkas painted with aniline are hung and sold in souvenir shops and have become far better known than the older scrolls that bore such warm natural colors.

# Thangkas

To prepare a thangka, traditionally, coarse cotton cloth—more rarely, linen, silk, or leather—was first treated with an undercoat, a mixture of chalk and lime. The linen was then stretched over a wooden frame for painting. A network of outlines was sketched in to make sure that the proportions of all the elements of the picture would allow the main figure to stand out appropriately, given the ideals of the order to which the painters belonged. In the next step, the painter—who was not necessarily the same person as the draftsman—filled in the broad areas with colors and then again had the draftsman sketch the outlines around scenery and figures. Once the eyes of the figures were set in, probably the most difficult part of the process, and one which was left to a spiritual master, work on the actual picture was finished. Only after the completion of the eyes did the picture become a dedicated image.

Another artist now had the job of framing the picture. First a yellow and then a red silk edging was attached; these symbolized the force emanating from the painting. Then a multi-colored, patterned border of silk was sewn around the entire painting. A rod was attached to the top so that it could be hung, another to the bottom so that it could be rolled up, or to weigh down the hanging picture. A so-called "door" of patterned golden brocade, whose meaning is unclear, was sewn to the lower hem of the border and marks authentic thangkas. In addition, authentic thangkas have many inscriptions on the back; these might be a description of the painted figure, directions regarding where in the monastery the painting should be hung, a dedication to the benefactor, a magic saying, or a monastic seal. In rare cases, the painting may bear the handprint of the lama who carried out its ritual blessing. It is only after consecration by the lama that the thangka becomes a cult painting.

Thangka with Dakinis. Tibet, 19th c. Dakinis or 'Wanderers in Heaven', as they are called in Tibet, go about as messengers of liberation. Equipped with supernatural abilities, they initiate the seeker, especially the yogi, into secret, mystic knowledge, whereby their often terrifying exterior is meant to ward off demons. In meditating on this thangka, which shows the seven Dakinis dancing in flaming aureoles, the believer should profit from the spiritual help given by these cosmic-wanderers.

## The Indian mission

Reports of the mission of Mahinda, son of the Emperor Ashoka, on the island of Lanka (see page 56) indicate that, by the 3rd century BC, Buddhist teachings had spread beyond the present-day borders of India. More defininitive evidence of the chronology of the expansion of Buddhism is offered by the edicts of Ashoka engraved in stone in several sites in what is now Pakistan and Afghanistan. In both these countries, Buddhist centers arose soon after Ashoka's reign, specifically the cities of Gandhara in Pakistan at the foot of the millennia-old route and Bamiyan, in Afghanistan, passing over the "roof of the world."

The Buddhist mission to Southeast Asia, on the other hand, set out from the coastal region of eastern and southern India. Trading ships probably ventured out as early as the year 0 from Kalinga (Orissa) and Andhra, although it is not likely that they bore any of the Buddhist teachings with them at this time. They did, however, bring Indian culture to a wider sphere, and this no doubt eased the later spread and acceptance of Buddhism.

During the 5th century AD, Buddha images appeared on the islands of Indonesia. At the same time, there were reports of the spread of the Hinayana in Burma. The later flowering of Buddhism in the more remote areas of India probably had something to do with the interest piqued among the Thai immigrants, while Indonesia drew its inspiration for hundreds of years directly from the Buddha's homeland on the Indian subcontinent; by the 7th century, there is written evidence from Indonesia

Bronze sculpture of Akshobiya, made in Bihar, north India, found on Java, Indonesia. Bronze, 8th/10th c.

of the Hinayana, the Mahayana, and the Tantras, the latter especially evident on Sumatra. The monastery Nalanda in Bihar (see photo page 79), India, was instrumental in spreading information, as the ruling family of the Pala dynasty (770–1095) conducted active sea-trade with the Indonesian archipelago. Most likely, however, Buddhism attracted its followers most among the upper classes of Java, where ancestor cults and Shivaism flourished among the people. With the decline of the Pala dynasty, contact with India diminished and Indonesia's dominant religious practice turned into something of mixture of Hindu, Buddhist, and animistic beliefs. To put it concisely, religious life was determined by syncretic teachings until, from the 14th century on, it fell under the domination of Islam. Overall, then, the mission from India to southeast Asia seems to have had very little influence on the Far East; in fact, with the exception of Vietnam, no geographic points of contact between the two great lines of development of Buddhism can be drawn.

Around the time of the birth of Christ, the relatively short-lived Kushana empire, during which period a vast area from the northwest of the Ganges to central Asia was dominated by the invaders from the north, set the stage for the northward spread of the teachings. This influence of the Kushana kingdom was felt not only in northern India and parts of Afghanistan, but also in regions beyond the Karakorum Mountains (see page 158). Within the far-flung boundaries of this empire, any number of cultural contacts became possible. Manichaeism and Nestorian Christianity developed side by side with Buddhism, which was represented in central Asia in both its Hinayanan and Mahayanan forms. Ultimately, however, the Mahayana proved to be the more enduring.

The great trade routes that led through Gandhara and Afghanistan would have allowed Buddhism to spread into the West, but the rise of the Sassanid

Buddha under the Bodhi tree (see photo page 17), above, a stupa; chiseled into rock along a route used by caravans traveling to China; near present day Thalpan Bridge, north Pakistan, 6th/7th c.

**573**
Buddhists persecuted in China
**581–618**
North and south China united under Sui Dynasty
**after 6th c.**
Own schools in China
**604**
Buddhism in Japanese constitution
**618–906**
Tang Dynasty, heyday of Buddhist art
**629–645**
Chinese monk Xuanzang in India
**7th c.**
First Buddhist mission to Tibet
**668–935**
Silla takes control over the other two Korean

Sogdian benefactors bring donations to the Buddha. Copy of a mural drawing in Bezeklik on the silk route.

dynasty in Iran (3rd to 7th century) fostered the growth of a nationalistic spirit, a spirit characterized by a distinct xenophobia. Where the exchange between East and West had flourished for centuries along trans-continental routes, the Sassanid mistrust of foreigners brought such intercourse to an end. As a result, trade across the mountain passes to Turkestan intensified. The oases along these routes grew from simple rest and exchange stops to splendidly appointed cultural centers. It is along these routes that one can find important Buddhist cave monuments with exquisite murals created over the centuries. For their models, artists used the paintings and small sculptures carried by monks from India. Most important, missionaries brought with them their holy writings, which were translated in these new

Scribes in caves of central Asia. Detail from a mural in Kara Shahr, ca. 6th c.

Trader along the silk route. Chinese glazed sculpture from the Tang era (608–918).

scholastic centers into the many the languages common to the region.

Thus Buddhism finally reached the eastern terminus of the trade routes: China. Buddhists in China claim that one of their own emperors was responsible for their contact with the new religion. Supposedly around the year 65 AD, this ruler dreamed that he should bring Buddhist missionaries from central Asia into his capital, Lo-yang. This legend is no doubt an invention of later generations, although the time frame is approximately accurate: During the later Han dynasty (9–220), the Chinese knew of Buddhist centers in central Asia and the first missionaries from India were received, albeit with very little fanfare. Nevertheless, Buddhist texts were soon translated into Chinese. The translations were generally not literal, owing in part to the reading habits of the translators who used stylistic elements from their native literature, and in part to the fact that few of Buddhism's abstractions had any counterpart in the Chinese language. The new religion demanded a new vocabulary, although some Daoist terminology was used (see below).

During the 4th and 5th centuries, well-known Indian missionaries made their way to China. Among these was Kumarajiva (344–413), who made new and

**1191**
Chan reaches Japan, where it is called Zen
**12th/13th c.**
Japan: Amida cult popular
**1206–1236**
Mongols invade Korea
**ca. 1215–1220**
Mongols conquer east Turkestan and north China
**1222–1282**
Nichiren Daishonin in Japan
**1279–1368**
Mongols rule over all of China
**13th c.**
Tibetan Sakya-pa takes over leadership in Tibet under Mongol supremacy
**1357–1419**
Tsongkhapa, founder of Tibetan Gelug-pa
**1368–1644**
Ming Dynasty in China, heavy repression of Daoists and Buddhists
**1392**
Rise of the Yi Dynasty in Korea, switch to Confucianism
**1576**
Mongols adopt Lamaism, in return they convey the title "Dalai Lama" to the leader of the Gelug order
**after 1603**
Tokugawa shogunate in Japan, foundation of new Buddhist schools only with official permission
**1644–1911**
Qing Dynasty in China, repression of Buddhists aggravated
**1720**
Chinese conquer Tibet

**1769**
Japan adopts Shintoism, Buddhists persecuted; Nepal adopts Hinduism

**1853**
American fleet forces opening of hermetically closed-off Japan

**1868**
Fall of the Tokugawa shogunate in Japan, the re-installed emperor declares Shintoism state religion, Buddhists persecuted

**1875**
Freedom of religion in Japan

**1912/1913**
Tibet independent from China; conference of Simla

**1921**
Communist revolution in Mongolia, Buddhists persecuted

**1950/1951**
Tibet invaded by China; beginning of sinozation of Tibet

**1951**
In Freewood Acres, NJ, USA, first foundation of a Gelug-pa community

**1959**
14th Dalai Lama flees to India

**1966/1967**
Numerous Tibetan monasteries destroyed during the Chinese cultural revolution, monks are secularized

**1987**
Chinese troops shoot at Tibetan monks demonstrating peacefully, after a phase of tolerance renewed repression of Lamaism

In Dunhuang, the northwestern Chinese endpoint of the central Asian silk route, the famous Magao Caves offer an incomparable ensemble of Buddhist painting and sculpture.

authentic translations of texts of the Mahayana, including the Lotos Sutra, which became extremely important in East Asia. At the same time, Chinese pilgrims made their way to India to the places where the Buddha had lived and to study the teachings of the Master in his native country. Among the best known of these pilgrims were Faxian (traveled 399–414), Xuan-zang (629–645), and I-ching (671–695). When they returned to China, they distinguished themselves as commentators and strengthened the native Buddhist schools with their well-grounded knowledge. The Chinese schools, in turn, were influential in Korea and Japan.

With the advance of Islam, however, the era of trade between India and its Asian neighbors ended. The stream of devout pilgrims from China died out, and the importance of Buddhism in its homeland diminished in equal measure.

### Buddhist synthesis with the religions of China

Buddhism's encounter with China was probably the greatest test in its history thus far, for it was in China that the teachings met an equally advanced, equally cultivated civilization. This is probably why so many centuries passed before Buddhism's influence was felt. Moreover, the Chinese at first saw little sense in the new path to salvation, which grew out of the Indian world view, of an eternal cycle of suffering. The Chinese were oriented to this life; they held a linear, historical world view in which great value was placed on exact historical chronicling. In such a context, propositions about the possiblities of liberation from ineluctable cycles seemed extraneous at best.

The centuries-old objections to Buddhism among the Chinese, then, is readily understandable: Buddhist monks engaged in no recognizable service to the well-being of the state; in fact, they barely managed to perform any kind of productive work at all, and took no clear political position. This made them seem dangerously fickle. Worst of all, Buddhists refused to participate in the ancestor cult that was so important in China: Ancestor worship was a part of the Chinese historical consciousness, which considered that the fate of all depended on its proper observance.

The ancient Chinese believed in the duality of a feminine (*yin*) and a male (*yang*) principle; this was a part of every macrocosmic or microcosmic process. The unity of the two formed the *tao* (also *dao*—"way," "teaching"), an all-encompassing order. In pre-Buddhist China, therefore, everything turned around uniting polarities in the sense of the highest dao, finding a resting point or balance between conflicting or opposite poles, as in an ultimate monism. It was particularly important to unite the human dao with the heavenly dao. This was expected of a virtuous emperor, who was believed to be the mediator between the here and the beyond, between earth and heaven. In this world view, pious actions, respect for those who were older or who had a higher social position, shaped society and determined the attitude toward

Daoism sees in yin-yang a universal law at work in both the macro and microcosm.

Chinese house altar. The Buddha Amitabha (set back) rules the composition with its many figures. Fire-gilded bronze, dated 584.

**Daoism:** Only little is known about Lao-tse, the founder of Daoism. While in the past he was believed to be a contemporary of Confucius, today it is considered more likely that he lived around 300 BC. The legend of his birth, which might have been taken over from India, is similar to that of the Buddha—with the consequence that in China both philosophers were often seen as identical. Lao-tse was a man from the south, rather a mystic in opposition with the moralist and rationalist Confucius who came from the north. Dao, the highest goal, according to Lao-tse, was a mystical quality and not, as Confucius claimed, the manifestation of a divine will. The ultimate reality for Lao-tse cannot be grasped intellectually, but only experienced in one's own life. To fit into this order is *de*. It means most of all a simple life in harmony with nature and thus denies the divine character of the state as taught by the ancient understanding of the empire. Instead of trying to be decent and fulfill one's duties, one should strive for *wuwei* ("not-acting"), i. e. do nothing that contradicts nature.

Daoist Magic Script: left, a sign protecting the body, based on the ideogram for "life" …

… right, a magic sign to fend off the black tiger of the mountains and the black fog

**Confucianism:** Philosophy going back to Confucius (551–479 BC) asking people to behave according to the Dao and be pious toward older people and those of a higher social status. The ideal is the noble human of virtue and education. Confucianism had its breakthrough during the Han era (after 206 BC) when people began to adore Confucius as a person as well. At first the cult object was the ancestry plate of the master itself, later on, approximately from the 13th century, his representation which was modelled according to the Buddha images. This fact caused quite some confusion in the West where both philosophies—as different as they might be—occasionally were taken for one and the same. In the year 1906 Confucius was even elevated to the rank of a major divinity in China.

ancestors. Naturally, observance of such an order generated elaborate rituals. The contrast with Buddhism could not have been more striking, especially when the Buddhist injunction against killing other living things is contrasted with cult rituals that involved human and animal sacrifice.

Daoism has several real (and some only apparent) parallels with Buddhism. One example is the meditative practice and techniques (breath control) or the emphasis on quiet as the medium of dao. These kinds of parallels enabled concepts from Daoist teachings to be used in the translation of Buddhist texts. These superficial similarites helped Buddhism overcome some of the initial difficulties it encountered in China, but they also stood in the way of its fundamental acceptance. For example, the Daoists, increasingly influenced by magical and alchemistic theories, sought in Buddhism some revolutionary method for prolonging life.

Colored Daoist stela, portraying Lao-tse as a divinity, has absorbed various elements of Buddhist art into its iconography: Lotos seat and lotos nimbus. Chinese stone sculpture, dated 583.

Buddhist teachings first escaped the pitfall that lay somewhere between disregard and misunderstanding in the face of political changes that came at the end of the Han dynasty (202 BC–220 AD). Around this time, the nomadic tribes overrunning northern China sought in Buddhism a spiritual means of countering what seemed to them the arrogance of Chinese culture, of Daoism and Confucianism. During the Wei dynasty (386–535), Buddhism first achieved prominence in China. Even in the south, where the "barba-

Early Chinese Buddhist manuscript. Each of the vertical columns is illuminated by two Buddha images.

rians" from the north had not yet arrived, interest in the philosophical and metaphysical aspects of the foreign teaching grew, and it soon became plain that new spiritual perspectives and dimensions were being suggested.

This development, however, destroyed the former accommodation between the Buddhists and the Daoists. Buddhist relations with followers of Confucianism were even more strained. In 445–446, a Confucian official in the north ordered the first persecution of Buddhists in China. A few decades later, discord again escalated when a southern emperor elevated Buddhism to the status of the state religion and forced the closure of Daoist monasteries and temples. These disputes, and the fact that Buddhism was practiced at court, seem to have generated a certain confusion and prompted rejection of Buddhism among the Chinese people. In any event, the teachings were reduced to a simple naive belief in the deliverer Maitreya (see photo page 12), commingled with ancestor worship and black magic.

At first, it was only northern China that had cultivated relations with central Asia and India, but, under the Tang dynasty (618–906), all of China was involved in the exchange, bringing in ever more Buddhist texts. Native schools were modeled on Indian schools or elevated one or another of the Indian teachings to their own special doctrine. In the Lüzong school, for example, strict obedience to the old monastic rules was the greatest goal, while the Wei school founded by Xuan-zang had a more philosophical orientation, devoted to the Indian Yogacara. In addition to Chan Buddhism, which will be treated separately (see pages 145), two other schools were important: Tien-tai and Jingtu. For both, the spiritual liberation of individual monks was secondary to the well-being of all. Tien-tai was based on the already mentioned Lotos Sutra, promising in this sense deliverance to all people: The Buddha nature was hidden within each individual and needed only to be

Chinese votive tablet. At the center of the picture is a 3-story pagoda, the Chinese form of the stupa, with Buddha figures seated inside. The scene refers to the 11th section of the Lotos Sutra, wherein a stupa with one of the Buddha's legendary predecessors inside, appeared to the Buddha while he was delivering his last discourse. Apparently, the Buddha finally sat down next to him in the lowest story. Clay tablet found near Xi'an, dated 650 or 656

found and cultivated. The Tien-tai denied any contradiction between the now and the hereafter, between reality and mystical vision; both comprise one perfect unity whose healing power could be experienced through meditation.

Jingtu, the school of the "Pure Land," had the oldest roots of all the different Chinese schools discussed so far. The "Pure Land" is the Western Paradise of the Buddha Amitabha (see page 73), whose cult had never really gained a footing in India. The school was already founded in about 350. Approximately 300 years later, Amitabha (in China known as Omitofo, in Japan as Amida) and his accompanying bodhisattva Avalokiteshvara (in China Kuan-yin, a female figure) had become the leader, or chief, of all bringers of compassion. The prospect of attaining paradise was clearly more popular than the abstract idea of nirvana. Better yet, the path to paradise was simple enough: To obtain the compassion of Omitofo, one had only to call out his name. Unfortunately, this formula seems to be based on an erroneous translation of a concept in the Sutra.

Head of a bodhisattva made of white marble in the Chinese Tang era style. Found near Xi'an, dated around 760.

Confucius and Lao-tse protect the youth Siddhartha. Chinese silk painting, 14th c., an allegory for the desired peaceful harmony between the different Chinese religions.

In 751 the powerful Chinese nation suffered a terrible defeat at the river Talas. Islamic forces advanced as far as western Turkestan and routed the troops of the Tang dynasty, indirectly ending Buddhism in central Asia. A defeated China withdrew into isolation and turned back to its own cultural heritage, to Daoism and Confucianism. The demise of Chinese Buddhism did not come about overnight; at first it remained untouched by the retreat to the older religions. The Buddhist

Monks in the Jade Temple of Shanghai. Even under the Chinese communists, Buddhist traditions have continued to exist, albeit in a modest form.

This depiction of the Dharma (see also illus. page 41), a work by the great Korean painter Kim Myong-guk, who supposedly only painted when intoxicated with wine, is so impressive because of the spontaneous lightness of the sketched lines. Ink on paper, 17th c.

monks had accumulated a fair amount of wealth and power, they had monastic slaves at their disposal and possessed large tracts of land, and they even functioned as bankers. Such excesses of monastic independence were cited by Confucian officials in the 9th century to sway the emperor in their favor, at Buddhism's expense. The result was a great wave of Buddhist persecutions between 843 and 845: Monasteries were expropriated, monks and nuns were stripped of the status appertaining to ordination, and almost 45,000 Buddhist buildings were destroyed.

Although the state later tempered its position, Buddhism in China never fully recovered from this blow. Confucianism, which in the meantime had absorbed a great share of Buddhist thought, clearly came to predominate. Interest in Buddhist philosophy waned, and benefactors were scarce. Both the Ming (1368–1644) and the Qing (1644–1911) dynasties waged massive campaigns of reprisals against Buddhism, and against Daoism as well. The imperial concern with political order even permitted only a compliant, diluted version of Confucianism.

A brief, rather weak renaissance of Buddhist teachings emerged in the early 20th century as a result of the pressure on China applied by the European powers. But the communist victory left Buddhism virtually no room to develop. During the Cultural Revolution (which began in 1966), many Buddhist centers were systematically destroyed. Only a kind of popular synthesis

survived, with the figures of the Buddhist pantheon assigned the role of talismans, to bring good luck, and with monks used now only as (paid) priests to officiate at for funerals or to predict the future.

## Across Korea to Japan

When Buddhism began to attain prominence in China, Korea was, culturally speaking, still at a neolithic stage of development. The country was divided into kingdoms: Paekche, Koguryo, and Silla; in addition—as the gateway for foreign influence—there was a Chinese province in the north. Between 372 and 528 AD, the three Korean kingdoms, in which until then only spirit and ancestor cults had flourished, embraced the Chinese models of Buddhism. During the Koryo dynasty (935–1392), when Korea emerged as a unified state, Buddhist teachings, especially Chan Buddhism (see page 145), flourished. However, in the 13th century, when Mongolian tribes conquered the country, most of the Buddhist monasteries and temples of this early period disappeared.

With the rise of the Yi dynasty in about 1392, Korea again followed the example of China and espoused Confucianism. Although a portion of the Korean population today still considers itself Buddhist, their religion amounts to a popular form of the teachings, infused with ancestor worship, and has acquired little dynamic force. One exception is Won Buddhism (*won* meaning "circle"), an order that actively undertakes charitable works. Its symbol is a black circle against a white background. Won Buddhism sprang up at the beginning of the 20th century, and, although it attracted many followers in Korea, it failed to draw much international attention. Korea's significance in the history of Buddhism, thus, essentially derives from its role as a mediator. From Korea, the missionaries set out for Japan. In 552, Paekche monks made their way to Japan to spread the new teaching. Japan in the 4th century was not unlike Korea, culturally; if anything, because of its insular nature, Japan was even less culturally developed

**Shinto**: Collective term to distinguish the specifically Japanese form of Buddhist belief. Shinto cults are ultimately all based on the adoration of nature; i. e. mountains, trees, etc. are considered holy places. The cult of the forefathers, a phenomenon found in large parts of eastern Asia, is probably a later development. In this context, already in pre-Buddhist times shrines were built in which the village communities adored their deities (*kami*).

According to Shinto teaching, the world owes its creation to the progenitors Izanagi and Izanami who also begot the gods. The grandson of the sun god Amaterasu supposedly was the founder of the Japanese empire. The first *tenno* (emperor) of Japan is traced back in direct line to Amaterasu as well, indicating that Shintoism does not recognize any contradiction between this world and the world beyond.

Monk of the Kegon sect, meditating in the branches of a tree, in harmony with the "back to nature" trend of the Kamakura era (1185–1333). Japanese scroll, 14th c.

and had absorbed hardly any foreign influences. The cults of the local ancestral gods (*kami*), out of which Shinto eventually emerged, were well entrenched.

At first, of course, the ruling classes welcomed the cultural achievements that were part of Buddhism. Prince Shotoku (574–622) even incorporated the teachings into the constitution by which he ruled. Shortly thereafter, in 607, Japan sent its first legation to the Chinese court. This became a custom that was followed as late as 838. It guaranteed regular exchange between the two countries of Buddhist monks and artists during this culturally significant epoch.

During the Nara dynasty (710–784), these relations with the Buddhist centers in China gave rise to six Buddhist sects in Japan: Hosso, a branch of the Chinese Wei-chi; Ritsu, a Japanese branch of Lüzong; Kusha, based on the Indian Yogacara teaching (see page 81); Sanron, a Madhyamika school (see page 77); Jojitsu, which followed the Hinayana direction of the Sautantrikas; and Kegon, which combined the worship of the Buddha Vairocana with the Shinto idea of a divinely inspired emperor at the head of centrally governed state.

Japanese scribes copying Buddhist texts. Their mouths are covered to protect the old texts from damage caused by human breath. Copy of a detail from a Japanese scroll of the 14th or 15th c.

Each of these sects embraced some particular aspect of the Chinese or Indian teachings—such as doctrines about meditation, magic, asceticism, and compassion.

At the end of the 8th century, the monks of the different Japanese sects that had all been established in

Nara had managed to accumulate such great political power that the emperor decided to move his capital to Nagaoka and, in 794, to Heian (today Kyoto). This move succeeded in significantly breaking the influence of the six sects, though a while later, two Japanese monks, Kukai (774–835) and Saicho (767–822), after a journey to China, founded two new sects; these would eventually become more influential than any of their predecessors. The Tantric school Shingon reinterpreted the native gods as incarnations of the Buddha; by this synthesis of Buddhism with Shintoism, the Shingon was able to give Japan some much needed political stability. The Tendai School (named after the Chinese Tien-tai), on the other hand, located on the mountain Hiei near Kyoto, demonstrated a particularly avid interest in political power. The hallmark of this school was its military style of monasticism, which spawned many mutually antagonistic sects. The Tendai even launched campaigns against other sects and engaged in armed conflict with the state itself.

Around the middle of the 11th century, times in Japan were extremely unstable, and would remain so until the beginning of the Kamakura dynasty (1185–1333). The Kamakuras ushered in a new, dynastically regulated era. It may have been the very insecurity of the times that stimulated widespread interest not only in Zen (see below) but also in a Buddhist movement that, because of its simplicity and clarity, had already won many followers in China—that is, the cult of the Buddha Amitabha (known in Japan as Amida). Because it was believed to be impossible to liberate oneself from worldly entanglements by means of one's own strength, it was necessary to trust completely in

Depiction of Aizen-myoho ("King of Esoteric Knowledge") in the form of the efficacious syllable Hum (see photo page 99), written in the Indian Siddham alphabet. Japanese hanging scroll, 14th c.

Fugen (known in India as Samatabhadra) was revered as the bodhisattva of highest wisdom, especially by the Tendai sect. Japanese wood sculpture with remains of gold painting, 12th c.

Amida's compassion. Hope lay in a rebirth into the "Paradise of the West." After this cult had produced numerous sects, Genku (called Honen Shonin, 1133–1212) founded a united Amida movement for lay believers that took the name Jodo-shu ("School of the Pure Land"). Jodo-shu ritual demanded unwavering faith and a pure heart to open the way to paradise, and consisted in tireless invocations of Amida: *Namu Amida Butsu* ("Honor to the Buddha Amida").

Genku's pupil Shinran Shonin (1173–1263) reformed the teaching once again: His Jodo-shin-shu ("True School of the Pure Land") held no direct expectations for invocations of Amida's name. Instead, he thought of the invocations as thanks to the Buddha. Followers were encouraged to change nothing in their worldly lives, to pursue whatever profession they pleased, to marry, not to worry about the principles of the teachings, asceticism, magic, or rituals, and simply to serve the world and the Buddha through their daily activity. This pragmatic teaching today still has the greatest following among Japanese Buddhist sects.

The movement of Nichiren Daishonin (1222–1282) was hardly less successful. He proposed equally simple "philosophic" demands, but his motive was clearly to

Nichiren, the Japanese founder of a monastic order, looking with his followers for a suitable location for a temple. Detail from a Japanese scroll, 15th c.

serve nationalistic ends. Filled with belief in the end of the world, he considered the Japanese people a superior race, for whom he wanted to secure worldwide recognition through the spread of his teaching. Nichiren claimed that the Lotos Sutra (translated into Japanese as *Myoho-renge-kyo*) was written by the historic Gautama Buddha himself and was the most important of all the teachings. It was, however, so difficult that his contemporaries could no longer understand it. Its content, however, he maintained, was actually already expressed in its title: Thus, continually reciting the words "*Namu-Myoho-renge-kyo*" ("Honor to the Lotos Sutra") was sufficient to gain salvation. Performance of such a ritual can no doubt produce a trance-like state, yet Nichiren was also a sharp critic of Amida Buddhism, which sought deliverance through the same method but used a different phrase. Nichiren's aggressiveness and fanatical attempts to win over the state to his own ends finally brought him to a sentence of death. He managed to escape, however, and spent the rest of his life in a monastery at the foot of Mount Fuji.

Fears that the Buddhist clergy with their militarized monasteries would grow too strong persisted over the next centuries, so much so that Oda Nobunaga (1534–1582) led a campaign against the monks of the Tendai School on their mountaintop. During the era of the Tokugawa shoguns (1603–1868), it was mandatory to obtain state permission in order to found a new Buddhist school. This period was characterized by isolation and fear. The country was hermetically sealed off from the outside world, since the shoguns not only feared internal forces and new civil wars, but also the diplomatic tactics and encroachments of the Portuguese. In 1853, an American fleet forced Japan to open its ports to trade. The

Bodhisattva Jizo, here as a mendicant monk with beggar's staff and magic jewel Tama in his left hand is for Japanese Buddhists the protector of children and women. Called Kshitigarbha in India, the transcendent bodhisattva was considered the protector of monks and those suffering in the nether worlds. Larger than life-size, colored wood sculpture, 1665

emperor was reinstated in 1868 and declared Shinto the only legitimate religion, although this edict was rescinded seven years later. Since then, Buddhism has continued to find new followers, although some renewed efforts were made during World War II to enforce Shinto.

At the beginning of the 20th century, the industrialization of Japan and its ascendancy as a world trading power were accompanied by growing national pride; this was especially conducive to the growth of the school of Nichiren. Several sects arose, building a quite modest doctrine out of borrowed fragments of Buddhist teachings. Some were of dubious reputa-

Japanese lay believers making a Buddhist incense offering.

tion. The Kokuchukai, for example, founded in 1914, was implicated in political murders during the 1930s, in an effort to force the Japanese government into an unconditional expansionist policy in the name of Buddhism. The Soka Kyoiko Gakkai, by contrast, were infamous for their unscrupulous recruitment methods: They were known to threaten families who had suffered mishaps with further disasters if they refused to join the sect.

**Right page, bottom:**
Buddhist patriarch Hui-neng tears up the sutras, to denounce the mania for scholarliness afflicting his contemporaries (7th/8th c.). Japanese hanging scroll, 13th c.

Meanwhile, most Nichiren sects pursue pacifistic goals; for example, the Soka Gakkai International (SGI) is active throughout the world organizing exhibitions, concerts, and lectures in various cultural institutions. The highly successful mission of the SGI (see page 182) combines historical inaccuracies and philosophic vagaries with a simple, easy-to-understand ritual of recitation. This cheap version of Buddhism, to which such prominent pop icons as singer Tina Turner feel drawn, always verges on exploiting people's gullibility for political or economic purposes. In such "schools," Buddhism has evolved to extreme forms that scarcely seem related to the original teachings of the historical Buddha at all.

Daruma (Bodhidharma) in an ink painting by the Japanese Zen master Sengai (1750– 1837). The master's commentary in the script to the left condemns the scholarly "wisdom" of Japanese Buddhists.

### From Chan to Zen

Chan Buddhism traces its origin back to a—possibly mythical—figure named Bodhidharma, an Indian, who supposedly traveled to China during the 6th century in order to teach meditation (*dhyana*; in Chinese, *chan*; in Japanese, *zen*). Nevertheless, it was Master Huineng (637–713) who first established an independent school that contains elements of Dao, of Prajnaparamita, and of Yogacara. Its basic assumption is that all creatures are unawakened Buddhas. To experience this as truth in an Awakening (in Japanese, *satori*) is the aim of Chan teachings. Four basic tenets—probably already formulated during Huineng's time—were necessary to achieve satori, and they are still valid today.

The experience of the satori takes place outside the written word. This idea had appeared in the Tantras, but Chan added a new aspect. Even for the Buddha, the so-called satori experience came about suddenly, in a precipitous contact with the reality of the cosmos. The

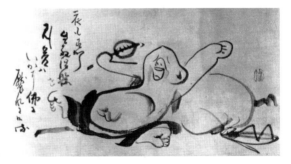

Refreshing awakening from the nocturnal "Buddha obsession." This ink painting by the Zen master Sengai (1750–1837; see illus. page 145, top) also affirms (in the sense of Zen) the spontaneous way to the Buddha-experience: Mere teaching is more of an obstacle than a help for Awakening to the self. Sengai's accompanying commentary is noted to the left: "All night I was tormented by thoughts of nirvana and samsara. Oh how exhausting the dream was. There can be no doubt, I was a captive of the Buddha."

Buddha had tried in his discourses to express this experience through images. When his words later became the object of research and study, interpretations began to obscure the spontaneous experience. Chan therefore rejected the commentaries as well as all the practices derived from them as a protest against a kind of learning that had become arrogant and presumptuous. In spectacular demonstrations, such as publicly burning wooden Buddha statues, Chan monks attempted to show their contemporaries the meaninglessness of rituals. The only thing that mattered was the reality of the moment. A Zen anecdote makes this point plain: Emperor Butei asked Master Fudaishi to give a lecture about a sutra. The master approached the lectern, but then he simply hit on it with a stick.

The meaning of this is that insight silences all concepts. And this leads to the second fundamental tenet of Chan teachings: Place no faith in letters. In writing something down, empty words—which are at best interpretations, at worst lies—become substitutes for direct experience. It is certainly significant that even during the earliest years of Buddhism, more faith was placed in the spoken than in the written word. Chan, however, fundamentally rejects all speech as useless.

Speaking, after all—and this is the third tenet—replaces the direct reference to one's own spirit. Chan masters try to prove that all dualistic thinking leads nowhere as they confront meditating pupils with seemingly contradictory or meaningless intellectual puzzles (in Chinese, *kungan*; in Japanese, *koan*). The contradiction, though, is only apparent. The point is to find—beyond all established patterns of thought—your own spirit. To experience what this "spirit" is—namely, not thinking, or a soul, or an empirically verifiable psyche, or something else—that is the essence of the Chan experience.

> "I do not like to hear the word Buddha."
> *Joshu, Japanese Zen master, 9th c.*

From this, the last tenet becomes clear—buddhaship is attained through direct insight into one's own nature. This "nature" must be recognized, perceived. It cannot be found through education, or through experience and the accumulated knowledge of a lifetime. It is inborn, the substance within us, the buddhahood to which our eyes must be opened.

In answer to the question of the path to this goal, the *Mumonkan* ("The Gateless Gate," one of the most important Zen writings) instructs: "The great Dao has no gate. There are countless ways to reach it." The disappointing first sentence, which seems to block the path from the goal, is dissolved in the second, through the change in perspective. Chan teaches no set way; each person must find his or her own.

If one considers the origins of this teaching, it is easy to understand why this is so. The early masters, after all, had no guides to copy or follow. They had to stride through the random and the uncertain, through a kind of dark night, to reach their goal on the other side. Teachers today warn their pupils that they will have to enter a "long night of unconsiousness" and will have to pass through deceptive, perhaps even pathological, stages of the spirit in order to experience satori. In short, they will have to survive death in life.

Study at a contemporary Zen monastery: It includes the necessary study of the writings and the disciplining of body and mind in meditative exercises. But the crowning achievement is the unplannable, unteachable self-contemplation of being (in Japanese: *kensho*), which is identical with the experience of Awakening (*satori*).

One frequently cited example of a satori experience tells the story of the Japanese monk Tokusan: After having practiced for years, Tokusan was sitting one evening with Master Ryotan, who finally made it plain that it was getting dark and Tokusan should go home. The pupil started out on his way but soon came back, since it was already dark. Ryotan lit a candle, but when Tukosan wanted to take the candle from him, the master blew it out with all his breath. The direct experience of darkness and light, of the source of darkness and the source of light, became Tokusan's satori experience.

A layperson would not have experienced anything terribly significant in this situation. According to Chan Buddhists, that proves that the only ones who can attain satori are those who have trained long and hard. Even though, in theory, many paths lead to the goal, empirical experience has been gathered for centuries, and today's masters try to impart this to their pupils as practical advice. Experience has also shown that there are some prerequisites to entering such training: Students must have religious longing, a strong will to undergo an intense search and severe discipline, and the readiness to face with courage the loss of self.

The persecution of Buddhists during the 9th century touched the Chan school far less than it did the other

Trainees in the Chinese monastery Shaolin. Today there is much ado with many tourists crowding in: The so-called *kung-fu* exercises, developed by Chan monks during the 5th and 6th c., are often misunderstood as mere fighting techniques, due to a number of popular films. The famous Bodhidharma/ Daruma (see illus. pages 138 and 145) according to Buddhist legend, was said to have spent nine years in the Shaolin monastery, staring in ceaseless meditation at the wall of his cell.

Buddhist orders throughout China. This was due at least in part to the tenacity and equanimity of the Chan monks, and in part to the fact that the monasteries were economically self-sustaining; the monks rejected begging for alms and instead farmed their lands themselves. Therefore, toward the end of the Tang dynasty, Chan attained a position of prominence that was surpassed only later by Amitabha Buddhism. Collections of texts from the 12th and 13th centuries survive, with the enigmatic sayings (*kungan*) that grew out of the satori experiences of the masters and were offered to pupils for meditative practice. The rise of the Ming dynasty, however, spelled the decline of the Chan school in China. Two Chan centers have remained important into the present: The Shaolin monastery near Lo-yang and the Temple of Cheng-du.

Zen monk during a concentration exercise.

During the 12th century, the teachings arrived in Japan, thanks to the Tendai monk Eisai (1141–1215), who had practiced meditation in China. The hostility of his former monastic brothers forced him to go to Kamakura, where he immediately earned great distinction among the *samurai*: Zen meditation exercises served as remedies for absent-mindedness and anxiety. They brought one equanimity toward death and increased the power of concentration. In this way, the samurai could perfect their skill in such un-Buddhist practices as the "art" of archery or sword fighting.

The Soto teaching founded by the monk Dogen (1200–1253) was a later variant of the Rinzai school of Zen founded by Eisai. Soto is the largest Zen sect in Japan, perhaps because the meditational practices of the Rinzai school are far more rigorous. Soto monks practice *zazen*, "spiritual composure while seated with crossed legs," and carry on *san-zen*, conversations about meditative experiences, with their teachers. These discussions are especially difficult since they require articulation of what are at their

The views of Zen Buddhism have been portrayed in widely differing forms of art, as in the rules governing flower arrangements or landscaping. For Japanese Zen aestheticism, it is essential that the "inner being" of all objects, surfaces or compositions be revealed in the "external" form. In

accordance, the Western observer is at times confronted with seemingly severe ceremonial aesthetics, forcing on the participant (for example, in the tea ceremony) firm rules that attempt to teach the participant as well as the observer respect for the autonomy of all being, even if only the simplest of clay bowls is involved. The deeper significance: The sense of the individual Buddha nature, (another inner being in an outer being) should be awakened in the creator as well as in the observer.

heart non-verbal experiences. Many disciples shy away from these confrontations, but if they show fear or hesitancy, they must endure the ridicule of experienced monks. This stern discipline is aimed at ridding the self of consciousness in order to see beyond it to the true nature of the spirit.

Once a year, in early December, Rinzai monks must submit themselves to an especially rigorous training. For one week, day and night, they practice zazen. Even the slightest movement is punished with strokes of the cane; thoughts and consciousness must be eliminated. The monks are not permitted to go to bed; they are allowed only a few hours of sleep seated in the lotos position. Such extreme practice ensures or proves that the Awakening can only be attained by a few elect.

Nevertheless, Eisai propagated a generalization that seems astounding to the West: Zen is not limited to Buddhism but is actually the center of all spiritual teachings. On the other hand, this statement is actually just a logical reversal of the fact that Zen dismisses all other teachings.

Chinese Chan, like Japanese Zen, has had a profound influence on art and culture. This is readily visible in East Asian painting and calligraphy, tea ceremonies, or the art of flower arrangement (*ikebana*). All of these activities and skills provide inspiration for the satori experience. Nevertheless, over the centuries, such cultural refinements again have served as substitutes for the immediate, direct experience that cannot be transmitted. Although he was a famous painter and calligrapher, it was the great Zen master Hakuin Ekaku (1685–1768) who warned of this danger. One of the most famous koans, which will close this chapter, comes down to us from him: "Do you hear the sound of one hand clapping?"

In addition to koans, the puzzles on which all dualistic thought must founder, Zen teachings also include an extensive catalogue of dialogues (*mondo*) consisting of questions and answers, as well as poems, popular tales, and other anecdotes. All serve the same purpose: To point out the direction to the student. Here are some examples:

A monk said to the Zen Master Joshu: "I have cast off everything. Nothing has remained in my consciousness. What do you say to that?" Joshu answered: "Cast that off too." The monk did not understand and repeated: "I told you, nothing has remained. What shall I then cast off?" Joshu answered: "Then you must continue to carry it." The meaning: The monk is on the wrong path, because he is boasting of his spiritual achievement. He must detach himself from his pride; but since he does not understand the admonition, he must continue to live with the burden.

With one hand, a monkey is gripping a branch that is hanging over a body of water, in which the moon is reflected. With his other hand, he is trying to reach for the moon, and will continue to do so unceasingly until his death. If he lets go, he will fall into the water and drown. The light in the ten directions is brilliantly clear. The meaning: As long as you are looking for the truth in something apart from yourself, it cannot be grasped. Insight consists in understanding that the truth is now and here.

Finally, without further commentary, a poem, simple to understand:

"The pine tree has a life of a thousand years,
The vine blooms for only one day—
Yet both have fulfilled their fate."

A monkey is looking for the moon in the water; but it is just the mirror image of the moon. Ink painting by the Zen master Hakuin Ekaku, 18th c.

## Early architecture: Stupa and caitya hall

Emperor Ashoka had the first Indian artwork produced since the Harappa culture. Famous are most of all the edict columns of polished sandstone on which the emperor, following an Achaemenid idea, promulgated the imperial teachings. The capitals carry symbols of Buddhism such as lotos, the wheel of the teachings (originally a sun wheel), as well as animal figures.

According to legends, the Buddha's ashes were distributed under eight mounds of earth after a dispute over his relics (see page 21). However, the emperor Ashoka, whose reign spanned from about 268 to 232 BC, supposedly had seven of these mounds opened in order to erect 84,000 stupas over the ashes of the Master throughout his entire kingdom (see page 50). Since 8 and 84,000 are symbolic numbers, the credibility of the report seems somewhat doubtful. In any case, hardly any traces of the burial mounds from the Maurya period (ca. 323–185 BC) remain. Certainly, clay or earthen mounds could hardly be expected to survive over thousands of years. More durable materials such as brick or stone were used for more important sites, while the original earthen mounds have been obscured by later additions, extensive expansions, and the continuous stream of pilgrims to the sites.

Stupa in the ancient royal city Vaishali, north India, with Ashoka pillar.

Nevertheless, two stupas in northern India provide interesting clues to early Buddhist architecture. One is in Piprahwa, not far from the Buddha's birthplace in Lumbini, Nepal. This flat brick monument, erected on a circular plan, originated from the time before Ashoka. Upon excavation, archeologists discovered enshrined within it a reliquary urn bearing the inscription "Buddha." Another stupa in Vaishali, where the Second Buddhist Council supposedly took place (see page 27), was expanded several times. Archeologists found at the center of the stupa a spot where it had been broken into, through which the relics were removed long ago.

Ashoka wanted the stupas situated not only in places where the Buddha had taught or at the intersections of important trade routes, but also on the sites of shrines dedicated to popular deities. In this way, local female and male native spirits (*yakshi* and *yaksha*, respectively) associated with fertility, wealth, and abundance, as well as snake gods (*nagas*) were integrated into the religion as protective spirits and soon became a part of Buddhist iconography. Accordingly, the reliquary containers in the stupas held not only ashes or remains of the Buddha (or of other monks important to the community), but later also devotional objects and votive offerings.

Temple frieze with gnome-like fertility genii or local vegetative goblins.

As burial mounds, the stupas symbolize nirvana, the unfathomable condition of liberation, that cannot be contained in words or images (see page 44). When you visit a stupa for the first time, you are immediately struck by how very much the ineffable has actually been captured in an abstract monument. A stupa can be categorized neither as sculpture nor as architecture: Formed on a geometric design, in which the past and future of human history seem to melt into one, it is a sacred monument that cannot be entered, only walked around. This circumambulation (*parikrama*), in which the worshiper follows the clockwise course of the sun and keeps the monument to his or her right, is the essential ritual performed at the stupa.

The famous Stupa I of Sanchi, central India, built during the 3rd/ 2nd c. BC, has four richly sculptured entrance gates (*torana*). It is one of the preeminent monuments of Buddhism.

Stupa I of Sanchi is a world-famous example of this early type of structure, dating from the time

of Ashoka, but enlarged (the radius was doubled) around 150 BC. The main body is here not as flat as in Piprahwa, but it is vaulted into a hemispherical dome symbolizing the cosmos. The circular plan of the foundation symbolizes the "Wheel of Teaching." By walking around it, this wheel is turned around the world's axis. The axis is represented by a pole that runs straight through the middle of the stupa; at the vertex of the dome this mast holds a three-tiered stone umbrella that serves as an honorary decoration or as a symbol of the stages of meditation. Under the honorary umbrella, there is an enclosed square platform (*harmika*), which was used in some stupas for the reception of reliquiae. A variation of the harmika was later developed in Nepal. Here, pairs of eyes were painted onto all four sides of the cubic harmika: The Buddha's eyes were to remain on the believers, walking around the stupa.

At Sanchi, the *anda* ("egg") arises from a raised circular platform (*medhi*), allowing a second circumambulation, in addition to the one performed at ground level. Both processional paths have high stone fences (*vedika*) that shield the shrine from the outside world. At each of the four cardinal directions, large, elaborately carved entrance gates, positioned

Votive stupa. Slate sculpture from Gandhara, north Pakistan, ca. 3rd c. AD. The dominance of the crowning honorary umbrellas and the dimensions of the foundations on which the anda is raised are characteristic features of the regional style of Gandhara.

The "all-seeing" eyes of the Buddha on the gold-plated square top above the anda of the stupa of Swayambunath, Nepal. The written sign for "1" between the eyes is usually interpreted as the symbol for the one true way to liberation.

like the arms of a swastika, lead to the circumambulatory path around the stupa and "thread" the
pilgrims into the correct ritual circumambulation.
This "entry into the stream" (see page 38) leads on
to a higher stage, to the circular path on the second
level. The stupa thus leads from the world of appearances to the heart of the teaching, from ground level
to higher spheres, a symbol of the desired spiritual
ascent. Later structures in southern India were no
longer massively constructed. Instead, invisible from
the outside, a system of supporting walls in the form
of a mandala (see page 104) suggested further
affinities to the teachings and the cosmos.

A stupa did not have to fulfill the usual architectural requirements of a building because it was primarily a monumental sacred object (*caitya*) and, as
such, was often sur-
rounded by a protec-
tive assembly hall. At
the beginning, these
halls were merely
round wooden struc-
tures that housed the
stupa and were occa-
sionally connected to
a square room for
community worship.
The linking of the

rounded area housing the stupa and the square
assembly area formed an apsidal-ended hall. Rows of
columns ran along either side of the larger halls, creating a circumambulatory aisle around the perimeter
of the structure and the enshrined stupa.

Early wooden caitya halls have not survived. However, their form can be surmised from various contemporary rock-cut caitya halls in which features of
these wooden prototypes are still apparent. The Deccan, in particular the area around Bombay, was well
suited to such rock-cut and grotto architecture. Buddhist cave temples had been built here since the 2nd

The Chaitya hall in cave
26 of Ajanta, central
India, early 7th c. The
surrounding columns
end in an apse-shrine,
suggestive of a stupa
and containing a
colossal Buddha image
(see photo page 173).
The Buddha residing in
the stupa has been
transferred to the
outside.

century BC. The oldest caitya hall (about 50 BC), in the apsidal plan described, can be seen in Bhaja; more famous, however, are the caves of Ajanta, which were adorned with beautiful sculptures and murals. Some scholars consider the Buddhist rock-cut architecture of Ajanta among the greatest of the world's art.

In addition to stupas and caitya halls, it is important to mention the *vihara*, the monastary, as an architectural type. Emperor Ashoka was already said to have had many lodgings for monks built, but they, like the early stupas and caityas, have not been preserved. Later structures follow a pattern that remained valid for centuries; this pattern used rows of small, modestly furnished private cells set around either a rectangular or a circular court (see photo page 79). A large assembly hall and dining area completed the simple scheme. This was gradually modified to fulfill new purposes: The courts were joined together to serve as a lecture hall, as lodging for pilgrims, as storage space, and so on. At the center of each court, a place of worship was set up and some cells were reserved for votive stupas or Buddha statues.

Stupa II on the western slope of Sanchi, central India. A stone fence (*vedika*) is set in front of the brick anda or dome; but its entrance gates, ornamented with picture medallions, are far more modest than those of Stupa I.

## From dagoba to pagoda

The stupa, as preserved in Sanchi, was a masterful symbol for the highest aim of early Buddhism. To ritually circumambulate the symbolic center of the world under the open sky and in bright light allowed the believer, on the one hand, to contemplate nature, to whose laws he was subject. On the other hand, the parikrama opened an inner sight onto a self seeking refuge in the teachings in order to find security in the cosmos. Here, need for protection was united with

The so-called Milk-white Dagoba (it was originally plastered with ground white shells) belongs to the monastery district of Alahana Parivena and has a 26-step crowning umbrella. Polonnaruwa, Sri Lanka, 12th c. Reliquary chambers have been found inside the dagoba.

the desire for spiritual growth. The caitya hall hewed these spiritual ideas deep into the rocks. Mountain and light, grotto and mystic darkness, the primal images of Indian metaphysics were brought together into their first art form.

Just as the early teachings only showed the way to a few, so complete understanding of its symbols remained confined to a small circle of believers. Soon the desire to contemplate concrete objects arose, and so, on the railings, gates, and foundations of the stupas, as well as on the mighty facades and assembly rooms of the caitya halls, an extensive pictorial program was installed: A reflection of the transformation experienced through the teachings, from the liberation of an individual through his or her own responsibility, to the liberation of humanity through the powers beyond.

Moonstones (*patika*) are placed in front of many Buddhist cult buildings in Sri Lanka: Semi-circular stone thresholds with decorative reliefs (flaming bands, animals, winding plants) picturing the world with its root evils. By taking steps into the empty interior of the moon-stone, the believer has taken a step forward on the path to Awakening.

Kushan prince with high felt hat. Sandstone sculpture from Mathura, north India, 2nd c. The Kushans had risen to the rulers of Afghanistan, north Pakistan, and northwest India as a consequence of central Asian tribal migrations during the 1st and 2nd c. AD. Their most powerful king was Kanishka.

Even in countries holding to the Hinayana, stupas came to be adorned with images of the Buddha, even though the architectural form and its symbolism remained traditional for a long time. The conjunction of image and symbol can be explained in part through the development of Buddhism from a philosophy to a religion, and in part through the stylistic traditions and the world view that these countries took over from their various Indian trading partners.

The dagobas (the word comes from *dhatu*, meaning relics, and *garbha*, meaning chamber) of Sri Lanka arose from the archetypal Indian stupa, but they are usually larger and are raised on circles of ascending terraces. The processional path can be reached by way of four flights of steps with semicircular thresholds, the richly carved "moonstones," placed at the foot of the steps. On the main structure of the dagoba are four projections, one in each of the cardinal directions, with altars or Buddha images for the purpose of receiving floral offerings. The height of the structure gives it a harmoniously flowing silhouette, like a "bubble," "drop," "bell," or "mound of rice."

Until the 4th century, Sri Lanka mainly took its inspiration from the southern Indian cultural landscape of Andhra. But other Asian countries that converted to Buddhism took their inspiration mainly from north India. Architecture here went through a period of transformation, from the forms and symbols of the Hinayana to those of the Mahayana: From round and hemispherical to square and cubic. On the one hand, the cosmological diagram of the mandala, which as an aid to meditation formed the *raison d'être* of the structure, could be reflected more exactly in square structures. On the other hand, the new form could be expanded in area and height more easily than the round form. Finally, the message of the Mahayana, which now dominated Buddhism, was addressed to the people in general and pointed to the divine, so that it almost became necessary to distinguish the sacred structures more clearly from secular buildings.

**Right page, bottom:**
55 meter high main tower of the Mahabodhi Temple of Bodh Gaya, north India, a kind of steep pyramid, built in the early 6th c.

The Kushan kingdom played a key role in the development of Buddhist art during the first centuries AD. The kingdom stretched from southern-central Asia to central India, from Afghanistan to Bihar, and possessed such cultural centers as Gandhara (a region in northwest Pakistan) and in Mathura (north India). Contemporary cultural movements inevitably flowed together at this political junction and the meeting proved productive.

In Gandhara, dominated by the Greeks since the Asian campaign of Alexander the Great and now trading with the Roman Empire, stupas were built on rectangular stepped terraces with flights of stairs at the four cardinal directions—a concept that had been adopted from the Near East. The medhi (the lofty platform that goes around the stupa) is stretched into a cylindrical form and has wall divisions in the provincial Roman manner, with Buddha figures in the niches. Sometimes several levels were constructed, adorned with reliefs depicting the life and previous incarnations of the Buddha. The path from the base to the vertex of the stupa thereby embodies still more clearly the ascent from the world of appearances to the Absolute. The "peak" withdraws from the earthly, as the top of the structure stretches higher and is adorned with a greater number of honorary umbrellas. The hemispherical dome, once the main body, has now diminished in relation to the base and the peak: The structure is gradually on its way to becoming a tower (see photo page 154).

A few centuries later, during the Gupta dynasty (from 320 to the 5th or 6th centuries AD), the

In Peshavar, the capital of Gandhara, there once was a tower-stupa, supposedly almost 200 meters high, which was considered a prodigy in east Asia and was copied many times. The anda here was reduced to a very small corpus between base and top. Supposedly, the Kushana ruler Kanishka built the tower over the first written canon of Mahayana Buddhism.

Buddha statue and bell-shaped stupas on the upper round terraces of the Borobudur beneath the central shrine.

tower as the image of the world mountain, Mount Meru, the mythical center of the universe, had come to be the epitome of a Buddhist shrine. At the Mahabodhi temple in Bodh Gaya, the stories of the pyramid-like structure taper upward toward the peak. Similarities to the earlier stupas are only vaguely discernible. Both Hindu temples and the high temples of the Pala period (770–1095) are related to this type, as in Nalanda and Paharpur: Ascending terraces built on a cross-shaped foundation bear a tower-like shrine that houses a Buddha (see photo page 84).

Such high temples, with various forms of spires over the central shrine, influenced Buddhist architecture from Burma to Indonesia. This development culminated in the Borobudur on Java (9th century). Erected over a mandala diagram, the temple has continuous reliefs adorning the lower terraces. On the upper terraces, small stupas were placed in concentric circles at the foot of a central shrine (see illus. page 104).

While the Indian paradigms were becoming known in south and southeast Asia, and the architects there oriented themselves by the structures of their neighbors, Chinese architects rarely had the opportunity to see the early models with their own eyes. If we judge by the monuments that exist today, it would seem that mostly cave temples were constructed in central Asia.

The most important sources for free-standing Buddhist structures in China were—besides the local style of building—reports from India, drawings, and votive stupas. We have only fragmented evidence about what was built as a result of these impressions, because, in the persecution of Buddhists during the 9th century, thousands of buildings were destroyed (see page 137). Nevertheless, the late form of the pagoda, as we know it, is at least partly based on the model of the tower-like stupa in India. The foundation here continued to increase in height, the stories were of uniform size, tapered only slightly toward the top of the building, and the surrounding ledges were widened into curving roofs. Under the high peak, the hemispherical dome still appeared as a symbol.

The Kumbum Chorten in the monastery Palkhor Chöde in Gyantse, central Tibet, dated 1440. Like the Borobudur, the Kumbum must be viewed as a three-dimensional mandala. By the ascending ritual circumambulation, the believer continually passes new shrines and divine images on the different levels. The peak of the stupa embodies the Absolute, the Adibuddha.

The polygonal building plan that was so popular in China can probably be traced to the local watchtower and appears only rarely in Korea and Japan. The Japanese rejected the Chinese pagodas of brick and stone, which were decorated with glazed roof tiles and colorful reliefs; they adopted instead simple, optically light wooden structures. They can be up to nine stories high, taller than their Chinese counterparts, but are built of materials that allow them to withstand earthquakes.

Stupas, caitya halls, and pagodas gradually lost importance in all Buddhist countries as icons increasingly came to represent the worship of the Buddha. The transformation to the tower temple that we have seen in south and southeast Asia is also an indication of this change. In east Asia, large Buddha halls became popular, built in a style based on local secular architecture: Saddle roofs with curved peaks and graduated gables. Once the separation of temple and monastic living quarters had been abandoned, these temple halls became the central shrines of the monasteries.

The empty throne and the footsteps signify the sacred presence of the Buddha. Such non-iconic depictions which do not show the figure of the Awakened One—here we see Mara's attack (see illus. page 17)—belong to the early phase of Indian-Buddhist art. Limestone relief from Amaravati, south India, 1st/2nd c. AD.

### The development of the Buddha image

The 7th-century Chinese pilgrim Xuan-zang made a surprising entry in his diary about his journey to India. About the capital of the kingdom of Kaushambi, he wrote, "In this city a monastery rises to a height of 60 feet, right in the middle of a palace; a statue of the Buddha made of sandalwood stands there, protected by a stone canopy. It is the work of the king Udayana." Udayana was a contemporary of the Buddha, and therein lies the problem. If this statue, as Xuan-zang reported, actually belonged

to the early period, then it remained an anomaly for centuries in the midst of otherwise non-iconic representations of the Master.

The oldest surviving reliefs—they date from the 2nd century BC—do not depict the Buddha; his presence is merely suggested through a symbol: The lotus blossom standing for his birth, the empty throne for his youth in the palace, a riderless horse for his departure from his parents' house, the Bodhi tree for the Awakening, the Wheel of Teaching for the first discourse in the Deer Park in Sarnath, a stupa for the entry into nirvana, and so on. This principle is often adhered to even when the *jatakas* (birth stories) depict the previous incarnations of the Buddha. The restraint shown, imbuing the pictures with a ghostlike aura, is the answer to a dilemma: How can the incomparable teacher be portrayed, who throughout his life refused to be revered and who in death—unlike other men—is totally extinguished and obliterated. Moreover, any image of this extraordinary man would encourage worship, which the Buddha had always maintained was an obstacle to liberation. This danger, however, could not be averted forever: Where the figures of worshipers are depicted around an empty throne, the godlike man to enhance the throne is not far behind.

The question of the oldest image of the Buddha ignited a scholarly conflict in which the Udayana Buddha, by the way, played no role at all. Instead, debate centered on the nearly insoluble problem of the chronology of the Kushans—the beginning of the Kushan period is variously set at dates between 78 and 225 AD. Gan-

Piece of a pillar from the early stupa in Bodh Gaya, north India, with a relief from the 2nd c. BC.

The legend of the fasting five. Glazed clay relief of Jataka, Pagan, Burma, ca. 1270. Jatakas are pre-birth stories: They relate the earlier incarnations of the historic Buddha. The often moralizing legends were only depicted with the sparest means as believers knew how to "read" the most cryptic suggestions. Here we see the later Buddha, sitting in a hermitage. As instructed in a vision, he acts like four fasting animals, whose lives had been endangered because of their desires.

Vajrapani, modeled on the antique Hercules. Stucco relief, Hadda, Afghanistan, ca. 3rd c. AD.

dhara and Mathura, the two cultural centers of the Kushan kingdom, both vied for the distinction of being the original location of the first Buddha statue. For a long time Gandhara was favored, as Hellenistic or provincial Roman elements of style seemed to prove that the work had been decidedly influenced by the West. For a while, its roots were even dated to the interregnum of the Hellenistic advance to the Indus. Nevertheless, the Gandharan Buddha, with the features of Apollo and set in the pose of a Roman emperor, probably only attests to the cosmopolitan spirit of the Kushans.

According to current scholarship, the first Buddha was probably created in Mathura, possibly toward the end of the 1st century AD, only shortly before the image from Gandhara. Inscriptions identify the Mathura

Sitting Buddha, sandstone sculpture from Mathura, north India, ca. 1st c. AD. The Buddha is enthroned on a lion pedestal and lifts his right hand in the gesture promising protection (*abhayamudra*; see page 171). As was probably fashionable at that time, the Buddha's hair is drawn tightly together into a braid. Left and right are Vajrapani and Padmapani as companions. Beyond the nimbus, the fig tree under which the Awakening took place can be seen. At the top, heavenly beings scatter blossoms.

Buddha as a "bodhisattva," referring to the early interpretation of this term as one for whom the Awakening was still to come. Even the followers of the Hinayana were able to accept an image that basically referred to the Buddha's existence in the world. The Mahayana, in the meantime, however, had developed a new interpretation of a godlike Buddha, one who should be worshipped and could therefore be depicted as an icon. The ensuing image was thought of as incomplete, as an illusion, a support for the path of spiritual meditation, but never as an embodiment of the highest truth. Consequently, both "vehicles" found their way to the image, but in places following the Theravada, the Buddha continued to have human-earthly features, whereas in places dominated by the Mahayana, his appearance was otherwordly.

Standing Buddha. Chinese limestone sculpture of the Tang era, 7th/8th c.

From these observations, it becomes obvious why the Buddha was first depicted in the Kushan kingdom in an era in which the Mahayana was beginning to flourish. This dynasty, arising from its home in central Asia, was used to thinking in terms of historical events and personages and had also taken over the desire to represent the power and importance of the state pictorially. In India, on the other hand, the belief in the cyclical nature of the temporal, encouraged an attitude of indifference to historical events. Nevertheless, in India, the Kushans came upon artists who were masters in fulfilling their desire for images of this world and the next. Thus, in Mathura and in Gandhara, an enchanting array of Buddha images were developed that sometimes owed more to Indian and then at other times to provincial Roman elements of style. A little later, in the 2nd and 3rd centuries, under the Shatavahanas, the great stupa at Amaravati in Andhra, India, also developed its own type of Buddha image.

The powerful Buddha figure of Gandhara did not become predominant in India, but, together with its wealth of narrative scenery, it did become the proto-type for representations in central Asia. Its influence foundered only in China, which had its own independent artistic tradition. Here, during the Tang dynasty, Buddhist art flourished and developed a style that exerted an influence on all other Mahayana countries of eastern Asia for some centuries. However, the carved wooden images begun in Japan during the 9th century are some of the few prominent examples of artistic production not dependent on China.

In India, the soft contours of Amaravati and, still more, the Buddha of Mathura became influential. There is no room here to analyze the style, but this Buddha image deserves special attention as a prototype. It was modeled on a very unlikely, pre-Buddhist deity, the *yaksha*, who, under the emperor Ashoka, came to be the guardian of the gate to the stupa (see page 152). The position of his body, viewed frontally, remained the position taken by almost all the Buddha images of Asia. His skin seems stretched, as though filled with *prana*, "vital breath," giving the figure a kind of organic strength and control, while nonetheless avoiding an athletic appearance. This depiction thereby anticipates later efforts to efface the differences between male and female, between polarities in general, in the figure of the Buddha.

Perhaps the greatest accomplishment of Mathura was reduction: Abandoning the plethora of figures in reliefs that were characterized by decorative images and embellished depictions. Narrative scenes teeming with life, in which the Buddha appeared as a symbol, grew into their opposite: Thus, a solitary figure in a symbolic scene came to embody an axiom of the teachings. At the same time, all efforts came to be con-

Buddha head.
Gilded wood sculpture from Tumshuq, central Asia, 5th/6th c. The so-called top knot of Awakening (*ushnisha*) lies under short curls, the "eye of wisdom" or *urna* between the eyebrows was broken out. Ushnisha and urna belong to the typology of the classic Buddha image, to the 32 great, suprahuman features of the Master.

centrated on endowing the Buddha's earthly body with an aura of eternity, and in furnishing it with the 32 greater and 80 lesser features (*lakshana*) that, according to tradition, characterized the more than human Master: The proportions of his body were "perfect" (as perfection was then defined), his shoulders wide, his hips narrow. When he was standing, his arms reached to his knees. Under his smooth skin, neither arteries nor veins could be seen. The fully rounded body of the Buddha, always depicted in a monk's robe, was replete with prana, the evenly, peacefully flowing breath of meditation. His earlobes were elongated, as still seen among Indian women today who have worn heavy earrings since early childhood. Siddhartha, however, had taken off all jewelry (once only worn by the nobility) when he left his father's house and became a wandering ascetic. At that time he had also had his hair shorn; thereafter, it never grew more than two inches long and is depicted in most images in short curls. An aureole, a nimbus, and his gold-colored skin make visible the sheen of wisdom and goodness, their light streaming from the *urna*, the mark between the eyebrows. The *ushnisha*, the top-knot, the sign of Awakening, crowned the Buddha's head.

During the Gupta period, the perfect rendering of this vision was achieved, first in Mathura, then in Sarnath, Ajanta, and Ellora. The fine-limbed Buddha of this time no longer looks directly at the viewer; instead, his lidded eyes appear to look inward with extraordinary peace. In his contemplation, he seems unapproachable, leaving his worldly audience with only one memento: to follow the path of meditation.

Sitting Buddha. Sandstone sculpture from Sarnath, north India, 5th c. This is one of the greatest creations of the Gupta style. The Buddha's hands are united in setting in motion the wheel of teaching (*dharmachakramudra*, see page 171), his face mirrors his deep introversion. Here, the spiritual moment is clearly emphasized in contrast to the rustic conception of the body found in the Mathura Buddha (see photo page 164), an older work by about four centuries.

The Buddha of the Gupta period reflects an iconographic and stylistic image that was accepted throughout Asia during the 7th and 8th centuries, and that may also mark the high point of Buddhist art. Nevertheless, the very perfection of this image increased the danger that artistic production would degenerate into mere reproduction. The first signs of this decay became apparent in India during the Pala era of the 8th to 12th centuries, and then made itself felt, despite interesting local variants, throughout the Buddhist cultural world.

Some art historians assert that creativity ceased around 1500: The artistic achievements of Tibet were—from the point of view of art history—only an insignificant finale. This Western scholastic judgment has no relevance for the believer, who uses the Buddha image for meditative and not for aesthetic purposes.

The monumental Buddha of Kamakura, southwest of Tokyo, Japan. The separate parts of the bronze sculpture were poured in 1252 and put together on the site. It is over 11 meters high and weighs almost 100 tons.

The extreme tolerance of the teachings, however, allowed continual room for changes, for new interpretations and special forms in the depiction of the Buddha. During the Pala era and later in east Asia, the Buddha was often depicted in princely attire, previously only donned by bodhisattvas (see above). This portrayal was based on the idea of the Teacher as world ruler. A far more impressive example of this idea arose during the 3rd century AD. At that time, in Darel, at the upper reaches of the Indus, a colossal statue was completed that contemporaries considered one of the wonders of the world. This colossus was often copied; among the most notable copies are, in Afghanistan, the two Buddhas of Bamiyan (ca. 3rd/4th–7th century), which were 115 feet and 170 feet high, respectively, and, in China, the 230-foot-high Buddha of Leshan (719–803). Colossal bronzes were made in Japan, including the 52-foot-high Vairocana in Todaiji (ca. 750); this bronze represents the achievement of an impressive technical feat—it took eight attempts at casting the figure before the final version was produced.

The reclining Buddha was a popular variation in Sri Lanka. The seemingly restful position of the Buddha was meant to emphasize the peacefulness of his entry into *parinirvana*; it was the last significant moment in the life of the Master that could be portrayed for the followers of the Hinayana.

In Gandhara, central Asia, China, and Thailand, another transitional period in the earthly existence of the Buddha became a focus for artistic activity, namely the asceticism that preceded the Awakening. These images are movingly real (see photo page 16). No less impressive are the great and famous heads in Bayon, examples of the Khmer art of Cambodia, in which the image of the Buddha merges with the idealized portrait of the king (see also engraving page 63).

The Buddha in *parinirvana*, at the transition from this world into nirvana. The 12th c. rock sculpture in Polonnaruwa, Sri Lanka, is over 42 feet long, and impresses through its realistic qualities: For example, the somewhat crumpled rock pillow in the middle and the curve of the finely drawn brows (see photos pages 172/173).

# Posture and Gesture

In Asian art, the Buddha is shown frontally and composition is symmetrical; only in situations referring to Siddhartha Gautama as bodhisattva is he sometimes turned toward accompanying figures and away from the viewer. Narrative reliefs or paintings with scenes from real life remain limited to lower stages of existence. Such scenes are often found on the bases of stupas or in the adjacent assembly halls. The images accompany the believer on his way to the Most Holy and prepare him for his encounter with the highest object of meditation by helping him call to mind the earthly stages of Shakyamuni's life or his earlier incarnations. In contrast, icons, considered beyond time and beyond the world, communicate with the viewer in a symbolic language that can clarify the image for the initiated and, at the same time, can arouse feelings.

**vitarkamudra**: This sitting or standing Buddha is like the *abhayamudra*, but the fingers point slightly downward and the thumb and index finger touch one another; in later iconography sometimes the left hand is pointed downward in the same gesture, symbolizing the ability to judge and reason.

The signs of this pictorial language include the posture of the standing (*sthana*) or sitting body (*asana*), the position of the arms (*hasta*) and of the hands (*mudra*). These gestures were developed into a perfect means of expression in Indian dance. In Buddhist sculptures, these positions and postures were developed in Gandhara, canonized in the late Gupta period, and then taken over by Buddhist cultures throughout the world.

The Hinayana makes use of only a part of the symbolic language, using signs to refer to one of the Buddha's historic acts (discourse, meditation, entry into nirvana, etc.). In the Mahayana and still more in the Tantras, these symbols serve to differentiate

Narrative terracottas in the monastery shrine of Paharpur, Bangladesh, 8th c.

**bhumisparshamudra**: The Indian seated position, the left hand in the lap and the fingertips of the right hand touching the earth, to symbolize the defeat of Mara, in which the Buddha called upon the earth as his witness.

# Posture and Gesture

**dharmachakramudra**: The Buddha is seated in Indian or European style, or sometimes is standing; his hands meet at his breast, the fingers of the left hand leaning against the right palm; there are many variations to symbolize the first teaching of the doctrine, or (through the addition of another symbol) the wonder of Shravasti.

**dhyanamudra** (also **samadhimudra**): The Buddha is always in a meditational position, his hands, one over the other, lying flat on his lap, symbolizing the moment of Awakening, but also meditation in general; in Japanese art the position of each of the fingers denotes a different meaning.

between the individual Buddhas and other mostly supernatural beings. If the right hand points downward (*bhumisparshamudra*), then, in the Hinayana, the scene of touching the earth is signaled: When the Buddha was beset by the demon Mara and was asked who could vouch for his truthfulness and courage, the Buddha appealed to the earth as his witness. In the Mahayana, however, this same gesture denotes the Buddha Akshobhya, who (like the earth) stands for steadfastness. In order to emphasize his characteristic trait, Akshobhya is given other symbols of firmness: A thunderbolt (*vajra*, or, in Tibet, *dorje*) that he holds in his left hand, and an elephant standing at the base of his throne.

Objects surrounding or held by the Buddha and symbolic animals denote an entire catalogue of associations that assist the worshiper in understanding the image. In Tantric Buddhism, the image or icon can have several heads or many arms and legs, to indicate omnipotence, and the arms can hold a number of symbolic objects or perform different gestures, disclosing the various esoteric qualities of the figure. In color representations—which are not restricted to paintings since most sculptures used to be painted—the color also symbolizes a further characteristic. Thus, Amitabha is the color red, whereas Siddhartha Gautama, usually almost indistinguishable from Amitabha in other ways, has gold-colored skin.

**varadamudra**: This is usually a standing Buddha whose right arm points down, palm and fingers extended toward the observer. It symbolizes compassion.

**abhayamudra**: This is usually a standing Buddha, right arm raised (in Thai art the left may also be raised, or both), open palms facing the observer, fingers pointing up, symbolizing the promise of protection, fearlessness.

Buddha protected by the serpent king Mucalinda. Sandstone sculpture from Lopburi, Thailand, 13th c.

Even the throne on which the Buddha sits plays an important role. The lion throne often seen in India is the symbol of a ruler and a sign of the teachings—the first proclamation of the teachings was likened to the roaring of a lion. The lotos throne, on the other hand, indicates Siddhartha's birth

and is also a symbol of purity. The seven- or nine-headed serpent, which in many sitting sculptures guards the head of the Buddha, depicts Mucalinda, the snake king, who protected the Master after the Awakening from a storm sent by Mara to torment him. Whereas the Buddha here sits meditating with crossed legs in the "lotos" or "diamond" position (*vajrasana*), a "European" sitting position (on a chair or stool, with legs extending downward, *bhadrasana*) denotes his active participation in earthly life. Sometimes, however, the future Buddha Maitreya is characterized in this way. If his feet are crossed, the figure is definitely

Again (see photo page 169) the Parinirvana-Buddha of Gal Vihara. Rock sculpture in Polonnaruwa, Sri Lanka, 12th c.

Maitreya, who calmly awaits his Buddhaship (the gesture itself indicates contemplative waiting). Another relaxed position, *lalitasana*, in which one foot is set on the ground and the other leg is pulled up, is usually restricted to bodhisattvas because of its asymmetry.

The reclining Buddha again shows how an understanding of the figure emerges out of the smallest details. The Buddha, like other monks, always lies on the right side of his body, with his head to the north, his feet parallel to one another. If the lower foot is slightly ahead, the position indicates the parinirvana.

Buddha, seated European style. Relief on the frontal shrine of the Pseudo-Stupa in cave 26, Ajanta, central India, early 7th c. (see photo page 155).

Whereas the Tantras returned, as it were, to the origins in that it "reduced" the Buddha, now the highest principle of the world, to a single symbol—for example, to a letter—Chan Buddhists went to the opposite extreme. They reinstated the Buddha as the historic teacher, depicting him without any special marks or symbols, and then destroyed this figure themselves without scruples (see page 145).

## Gods and Buddhas, bodhisattvas and demons, holy men and teachers

In addition to the Buddha of the Hinayana and the Buddhas of the newer schools, an immense and incredibly diverse pictorial and symbolic language evolved within Buddhism. In the old teachings, this complex language of images referred to the historical Buddha; in the Mahayana and the Tantras it also depicted cosmological theories; in cultures outside of India it even came to include figures from other religious systems. The artists of Gandhara chose different physiognomies, dress, and elements of style in order to characterize the different stages of being. This principle was carried over central Asia into China,

where it was finally abandoned. In Mathura, on the other hand, artists attempted to portray higher figures in an idealized manner and earthly ones realistically. In time this became the highest standard of Buddhist art and explains why, after the creation of a valid Buddha image, creativity and artistic energy were funneled into the creation of figures of lower beings, whose numbers then also steadily increased. Proof of this is to be seen especially in the late Buddhist art of China.

Death-dancer Chitipati. A companion of Yama, the Judge of the Dead. Silver plated bronze, Mongolia, 19th c.

While the Hinayana, true to its central premises, remained thematically limited and adopted demons and other supernatural figures into its repertoire only at a late date, Mahayana and Tantric Buddhism were continually developing new beings, due in part to cosmological speculations, in part to the adoption of popular cults. In so doing, they were extremely careful to classify the figures exactly so that they could be integrated into the rigid hierarchy of the levels of being.

Chinese good-luck figures, in the West often mistaken for images of the Buddha. Modern glazed ceramic.

The highest level, the Buddhas, is followed by the bodhisattvas. Like the Buddhas, these are spiritualized, idealized, and beyond gender, but they wear expensive jewelry to signify their solidarity with life on earth, and their posture is relaxed. They often take on a pose known as *tribhanga*, a threefold S-curving of the body, well known in Indian dance. This pose is most often used when two bodhisattvas flank a Buddha: Here the tribhanga posture—one figure curving to the left, the other to the right—focuses the viewer's gaze on the actual icon in the middle. In this case, the bodhisattvas are to be understood as accompanying figures, but, since the Mahayana reveres them as direct vessels of deliverance, they themselves were finally placed into the center of sacred pictures. This also happened to Maitreya, who evolved in popular Chinese Buddhism into Budai ("sack of hemp")—a fat, laughing figure thought to bring good luck and often mistaken in the West for the Buddha. Similarly, Manjushri, Tara, Prajnaparamita, and Avalokiteshvara evolved; Avalokiteshvara is often depicted with many heads and limbs (as the "eleven-headed one with the great compassion," see photo page 125), a trait that points to Tantric-Hindu influence. His popularity is clear from the approximately 130 iconographic variations of his person. Avalokiteshvara (in Chinese, Kuanyin; in Japanese, Kuannon) thereby continues to take on new tasks: He can even appear as the god

Fudo, one of the "Kings of Esoteric Knowledge" (see also illus. page 141). Colored wood sculpture, Japan, 12th c. Altogether there are five such kings. They are considered angry embodiments of the five Buddhas of Esoteric Knowledge and are supposed to force the hesitant and closed-minded to the path to liberation.

of other religions in order to lead people who have erred into the wrong belief back to the right path. He is the patron bodhisattva of Tibet. His many identities on the other hand led to Avalokiteshvara merging with the Hindu god Shiva, which meant that he lost his followers in India.

Just as the bodhisattvas stand for the compassionate aspect of the highest beings and act according to their behest in a benevolent way, so the "Kings of Wisdom" (*vidyarajas*) embody the angry element. These beings, which first belonged to the Hindu body of thought, were introduced later into the Buddhist spiritual and pictorial world. They are a typically Tantric feature, elucidating the Tantric need to find unity or the highest truth in the balance of polarities: Nothing and no one can be universally good or evil; the only truth lies in a Middle Way, a resolution in a neither-nor.

The level of the twelve highest gods is followed by a fundamentally different sphere, by the beings of samsara. They are given long lives, but not eternal ones, and for the time being they are also not destined for nirvana. In order to arrive at the highest goal, they first have to go through earthly existence and experience the suffering of life.

On the next rung of the ladder are the four "Guardians of the Worlds" (*lokapalas*; also called *devarajas*, "Kings of Heaven"), then the "Guards of Heaven's Gates" (*dvarapalas*), as well as all kinds of divine and demonic beings of different origins. They are easily recognized by their aggressive posture and ferocious expressions. In addition, they are depicted making threatening gestures, holding decapitated heads or wine-filled skulls in their hands and stamping with rage on gnome-like beings. All of this frightening cosmological imagery, stemming from

Hindu beliefs, metamorphosed in Tantric Buddhism into beings that combat the ancient causes of suffering: Greed, hate, and ignorance, personified by the gnomes.

Below the level of the lower gods and demons are humans who have not yet attained the Awakening. On the other hand, someone who has reached this highest stage of wisdom is, in the Hinayana, called *arhat* ("Holy One," "Guide"). His place is above the gods and next to the Buddha, whereas, in the Mahayana, he is given a place right under that of the bodhisattvas. It was the artistic quest for ways to depict someone who was in movement and gesture still earthly, but was in his aura already holy and a teacher that produced masterpieces of sculpture and painting during the late era of Buddhism in Tibet.

Special attention is finally due to the earthly-celestial pairings of the Tantrayana, shown in bodily union, known in Tibet as *yabyum*, and symbolizing the end of duality. It is perhaps precisely this motif of unity in love that best provides the key to the Tantric body of thought. In the West it has often led to fundamental misconceptions: Unknowing viewers see only an "intriguing" depiction of sexual intercourse and are unable to decipher the wealth of iconographic references.

All the figures have their firm place within a spiritual structure. This art is effective only in its context, sometimes only in the place where it was created and shown solely to initiates. To strip out motifs and context empties Buddhist art of its purpose and its significance. This is why Buddhist works displayed in museums often seem to lack vitality and immediacy.

The Adibuddha Samantabhadra with his prajna in sacred act of love (*yabyum*). Detail (center) of a thangka, Ladakh, 20th c. Samantabhadra as an original Buddha is always depicted naked. He and his consort Samantabhadri are identical with each other.

"When iron birds fly through the air, Buddhism will wander west and reach countries far away."

*Padmasambhava, 8th c.*

When the Portugese first landed on Sri Lanka in 1505, they were shocked by the fact that they found an unknown but clearly very powerful religion. This agitation soon led to armed combat and forced conversions. The Christian missionaries of this time left a far from positive impression of their teachings in Asia; their own reaction to the native cultures they encountered was mistrustful and colored by an almost grotesque ignorance. When, for example, in the 16th century, the first Jesuits were confronted with Amida Buddhism, they notified their order at home that Martin Luther's heresies had already reached Japan. Nevertheless, reports of the strangeness of the distant world stirred interest among scholars in Europe. Many thinkers and writers endeavored to reconcile their limited knowledge with Western theories, which propagated further misunderstandings. The reactions of Baron von Leibniz or of Voltaire to China are prime examples.

The German philosopher Arthur Schopenhauer (1788–1860) was the most prominent representative of this un- or pre-academic appropriation of Buddhism. Schopenhauer was convinced that his own world view already encompassed Buddhist ideas. Indeed, at first sight, remarkable corollaries appear: He proposed a negating-pessimistic view of the world (Schopenhauer, "Life is a miserable thing") that might be considered akin to the notion of life as suffering, and also professed a now-famous ethic of compassion. Schopenhauer ardently promulgated these seemingly compatible ideas, expressed a preference for the moral teachings of Buddhism over those of Christianity, and thereby called public attention among Europeans to the alien doctrine.

At the same time, British colonial officials, who started to learn the language, began to translate Mahayana texts into English. The first real surge of

Arthur Schopenhauer (1788–1860) writes in his main work *The World as Will and Idea*: "Everything in life gives evidence of the fact that earthly happiness is destined to be thwarted or to be recognized as an illusion." This and other insights of the German philosopher correspond to the basic tenor of early Buddhism with its rejection of the world.

interest in the East that also had a positive influence upon Buddhism in Asia began during the second half of the 19th century and coincided with the study of the Buddha's life and the early teachings from the Pali texts. The pioneers of this work were English scholar Thomas Williams Rhys Davids (1843–1922) and German scholars Hermann Oldenberg (1854–1920) and Karl Eugen Neumann (1865–1915), who produced brilliant

translations of the original texts. Under the auspices of the "Pali Text Society," founded by Rhys Davids, notable editions and translations of texts that are in many instances rare or even unknown in Buddhist countries continue until today.

Bust of Anagarika Dharmapala (1864–1933) on Sri Lanka is a reminder of the Buddhist revival movement at the end of the 19th c. and of the fact that its main impetus came from Europeans.

It was the American edition of the "Great Debate of Panadura" (1873) between Buddhists and Christians on Sri Lanka (1865) that led to the founding in 1875 of the "Theosophical Society" in New York by the occultist Helena Petrovna Blavatsky (1831–1891) and Colonel Henry Steel Olcott (1832–1907). The society—to which Austrian anthroposophist Rudolf Steiner (1861–1925) also belonged for a time—had two goals: To find the common esoteric supernatural center of the great religions, and to disseminate Asian teachings in the West. In 1881, Olcott published a *Buddhist Catechism* (1881); in 1890 he founded a Buddhist Theosophical Society on Sri Lanka and, a year later, with his friend Anagarika Dharmapala (actually David Hewavitarne, 1864– 1933), founded a society to maintain the monument Bodh Gaya and other neglected Buddhist sites in India. Although the

Helena Petrovna Blavatsky was one of the most glittering figures of Victorian occultism. In the 19th c., in which there were still "white spots" on the map of the world (for example, Tibet), the Russian-born Blavatsky maintained that she had spent seven years with the wise men of the Himalayas, and then she gave expression to her obscure insights out of these "educational years" by founding the Theosophical Society.

so-called Mahabodhi Society was highly successful in its efforts at such preservation, it was not able to revive the teachings in India.

In 1897, four years after the Chicago World's Fair which brought together for the first time representatives of all major religions to exchange ideas, an American branch of the Mahabodhi Society was established; it was the first Buddhist organization in the West. The first Buddhist society in Germany was founded in 1903, in Great Britain in 1907. In Britain, a wide range of Buddhist teachings sparked interest, and it was here that the idea originated of combining the different schools into a unified new movement, the Navayana, or "New Vehicle." In the United States, East Asian Buddhism was the best-known form; it arrived here largely via the waves of Chinese and Japanese immigration that brought laborers to work on the railroad since about 1860, and with the annexation in 1888 of Hawaii, which had been converted by Japanese Jodo-shin-shu missionaries.

Whereas the Theravada was almost unheard of in the United States, in Germany it was the focus of scholastic attention, almost to the exclusion of other schools. The Englishman Allan Bennet McGregor (1872–1923), ordained in Burma in 1902, was the first Buddhist monk from the West. The German violin master Anton Gueth (1878–1957) followed his example, becoming a monk in Burma in 1904, and then going to Sri Lanka as Nyanatiloka Mahathera. There, on a small island in front of Dodanduwa, he founded a monastery that attracted many Buddhists from the West, among them in 1936 Nyanaponika (Siegmund Feniger, 1901–1980), who, like Nyanatiloka, wrote a number of important essays on Theravada Buddhism and also founded his own publishing house, the Buddhist Publication Society.

After World War II, the number of Buddhists in the West grew rapidly. Two movements that

The Buddha in an illustration from *Das Evangelium des Buddha* ("The Gospel according to Buddha"), a work influential in the West, circulating in American and German editions from 1894. Olga Kopetzky's illustrations for the 1919 edition portray the Buddha as an object of Art Nouveau. It is impossible to overlook the iconographic similarities between him and the figure of Christ.

previously had hardly attracted attention now came to dominate: Zen and Lamaism. Americans came into contact with Zen Buddhism first through the war with Japan. *The Dharma Bums*, a novel by Jack Kerouac published in 1958, acquainted the Beat generation with this Zen Buddhism. Somewhat later, scholars such as Daisetz Teitaro Suzuki managed to interest a surprising number of readers for the basic tenets of Zen. Traces of Zen teachings can also be found in Friedrich Perls's Gestalt therapy, a subject that drew a great many young people into seminars in California. All of these events combined to make Zen—often completely misunderstood—a leitmotif of the Hippie movement. In the late sixties, various divergent Zen centers sprang up, for example, on Hawaii, in San Francisco, and in New York. An especially ambitious undertaking, the Sino-American Buddhist Association, was founded in San Francisco in 1968. Shortly thereafter, this Chan association established the Golden Mountain Dhyana Monastery and the City of 10,000 Buddhas in northern California.

Lamaism has a similarly large following in the West, including movie stars Richard Gere and Harrison Ford, who have been quite public about their religious interests. In addition, recent films such as *Living Buddha*, *Little Buddha*, and *Kundun* have focused interest on this movement. Tibet had already become the mystic wonderland of Buddhism for the Theosophists, but the Chinese invasion and the flight of the Dalai Lama to India in 1959 brought this country a new wave of international sympathy (see page 117). Many Tibetan monks emigrated to the West where they founded Lamaistic monasteries and other institutions. Switzerland became the center of Tibetan Buddhism in Europe. Chögyam Trungpa and Akong Rinpoche were especially active; they established the monastery Samye Ling (Johnston

Fritz S. Perls (1893–1970), one of the founders of Gestalt therapy.

Scene from the film *Little Buddha* with Keanu Reeves, directed by Bernardo Bertolucci.

House, Dumfries) in Scotland in 1967. Other institutions housing different Tibetan schools followed in quick succession, for example, in Copenhagen, where Hannah and Ole Nydahl diligently conducted missionary work, and in Hamburg, Germany, where the Tibetan center is especially distinguished.

In 1973, Trungpa set up the headquarters of a new organization called Vajradhatu in Boulder, Colorado. Here, Tibetan Buddhism mingles with Zen teachings, Gestalt therapy, and other ideas from the West and the East, attesting to the tolerance and enormous adaptability of Buddhism, qualities that have remained unchanged throughout its history.

The Soka Gakkai International (known in the United States as Nichiren Shoshu of America), originally from Japan, is perhaps the most popular Western Buddhist organization, partly because of the simplicity of its teachings and partly due to the missionary zeal of its members.

Is Buddhism in the West simply a fashionable trend, another consumer-oriented idea, to help assuage material and psychic worries? While it

Young western Buddhist novices in Bodh Gaya, north India.

may inevitably have come to appear a fashion, a Western spiritual placebo, the history of its development clearly shows that the phenomenon of Buddhism cannot be reduced to anything so shallow. After all, Buddhism drew within its sphere many Asian countries, including countries that already had highly developed cultures and advanced civilization. This was accomplished not through crusades, but through tolerance, openness, and the persuasive power of its philosophical foundations. In fact, its insights into time and space, including the concept of insubstantiality, have found some measure of corroboration in Western science. Truth and reality have been questioned under Buddhism in ways that Western philosophy has only approached recently under the influence of paradigm changes in the natural sciences. Significantly enough, such pioneering physicists as Nobel Prize winner Erwin Schrödinger (1887–1961) have praised the Buddhist conception of determinism and free will.

In order to understand the power of Buddhism, it is necessary above all not to mistake Buddhism for a religion with a dogmatic canon. Buddhism arose out of the profound psychological and ethical experience of a human being concerned about the fate of humanity, someone who wanted to be neither a god nor a guru, someone who intently and in the end successfully pursued a spiritual quest. All the manifestations of the teachings, regardless of where the different versions may diverge, bear the imprint of this initial quest. It is most important for every Western novice to remember this fundamental difference: The West has always sought eternal life, the Buddhist East, the end of the cycle of rebirths.

Buddha walks over the earth. The footprints of the Awakened One, decorated with the Wheel of Teachings and Buddhist signs for good luck; on a background of a lotos flower. Detail from a Nepalese thangka.

# Glossary

**Adibuddha**
Personification of the Absolute in later Buddhism

**Amitabha**
"The Buddha of Boundless Light," worshipped as Amida in Japan

**Andhra**
Ancient cultivated area in southern India, comparable in size to the present state of Andhra Pradesh

**Arhat**
"Holy One," one who has reached Awakening as the highest goal of Hinayana Buddhism

**Ashoka**
Most important emperor of the Maurya dynasty

**Atman** (Sanskrit), **atta** (Pali)
Man's "self," the individual soul striving to become one with Brahman, the world soul (*anatman*, or *anatta*, teachings are rejected by Buddhism)

**Avalokiteshvara**
Most important bodhisattva of the Mahayana, the embodiment of Infinite Compassion

**Bhikshu** (Sanskrit), **bhikkhu** (Pali)
monk

**Bodhi**
Awakening, Enlightenment

**Bodhisattva**
An Awakened being, a being who aspires to be a Buddha

**Bo(dhi) tree**
Fig tree (*Ficus religiosa*); beneath this tree, the Buddha experienced Awakening; also called pipal tree

**Brahma**
God of Brahmanism and Hinduism (the Creator), highest divinity together with Vishnu (the Preserver) and Shiva ( the Destroyer)

**Brahman**
World soul, impersonal law governing the world

**Brahmanism**
Early form of Indian religion; priests (Brahmans) had sacrificial rites and knowledge of the Vedas in their control, and therefore held leading positions in society

**Caitya** (Sanskrit), **cetiya** (Pali)
Pile of ashes, sacred object, shrine, temple, especially in the form of a rectangular hall with an apse

**Cittamatra**
A Mahayana teaching, asserting that the world is "mere thought" (*citta*); other terms for this school include *Vijnanavada* ("teaching of consciousness"), whereby the world comes into existence only through consciousness of it), and *Yogacara* ("change through yoga"), in which insight is sought through asceticism, magic, and trance

**Chorten**
Tibetan form of *stupa*

**Dagoba**
The form of *stupa* built in Sri Lanka

**Deccan**
Central Indian highland

**Dharma** (Sanskrit), **dhamma** (Pali)
Basic principles forming the foundation of all being; also Buddhist teachings; for Ashoka, morals

**Dharmachakra**
"Wheel of Teaching"

**Dhyana**
Meditation (Chinese: *chan*; Japanese: *zen*)

**Dhyanibuddha**
See *Jina*

**Gandhara**
Cultivated area in northern Pakistan

**Gautama**
Surname of the historical Buddha

**Gupta**
Dynasty in north India; patrons of Buddhism, art, and architecture

**Harappa**
Archeological excavation site in modern Pakistan; gave its name to a pre-Aryan civilization

**Hinayana**
"The Lesser Vehicle," the Old School of Wisdom, holding the prospect of liberation out to only a select few

**Jainism**
Indian teaching of liberation, originated at approximately the same time as Buddhism and founded on similar concepts. Highest commandment is *ahimsa* (not to kill), a commandment extending to all living beings

**Jataka**
Sacred legends of the Buddha's previous incarnations

**Jina**
"Victor," epithet for Mahavira, the founder of Jainism; in Mahayana and Tantrayana, the heavenly Buddha, earlier called *dhyanibuddha* ("Meditation Buddha")

**Karma(n)**
"Deed," good or bad deeds of current life, determining level of reincarnation

**Kshatriya**
Member of the warrior caste

**Kushana**
Dynasty originally from central Asia, migrated to India around the beginning of the 1st century AD, established a large kingdom with center in northwest India, supporters of Buddhism

**Lama**
Traditionally a religious master and spiritual

# Glossary

authority in Tibetan Buddhism, today used as a form of address for any ordained Tibetan monk

**Lamaism**
Tibetan form of Buddhism

**Madhyamika**
"Teaching of the Middle Way," one of the Mahayana schools, which has as its central doctrine *Shunyata* ("Emptiness"); most famous exponent was Nagarjuna

**Magadha**
Ancient kingdom in north India, part of the present state of Bihar; the Buddha was active here

**Mahasanghika**
Early or preliminary stage of Mahayana

**Mahayana**
"The Great Vehicle," New School of Wisdom with paths to liberation for everyone

**Maitreya**
The future Buddha

**Mandala**
"Circle," symbolic diagram of the cosmos in two- and three-dimensional form, used as a guide to meditation

**Manjushri**
"He who is noble and gentle;" the bodhisattva of wisdom

**Mantra**
A powerful syllable, word, or phrase recited as a form of meditition

**Mara**
Demon, ruler over the realm of death

**Maurya**
Important pre-Christian dynasty, patrons of Buddhism who expanded their realm from their original seat in Magadha to nearly all of India

**Maya**
Deception, illusion; name of the Buddha's mother

**Mudra**
Gesture, position of the hand with symbolic meaning

**Naga**
Snake, guardian of spiritual truths

**Nagarjuna**
South Indian reformer of Buddhism, lived around 200 AD, most important advocate of the Madhyamika

**Nirvana** (Sanskrit), **nibbana** (Pali)
Literally "extinguishing due to lack of fuel," dying out, the highest goal of Buddhism, suggesting that the body is extinguished because it is no longer fueled by earthly desires

**Pala**
Ancient dynasty in what is today Bihar and Bengal, the last patrons of Buddhism in India

**Pali**
Indian scholarly language, main language used in Hinayana texts

**Pali Canon**
The teachings of the Theravada drawn together in the "Triple Basket" (Pali: *tipitaka*), first written form in Sri Lanka

**Parinirvana**
Entry into Nirvana for the Awakened upon death

**Prajnaparamita**
Perfection of wisdom as a factor of liberation, a central concept of the Mahayana, personified as a female bodhisattva

**Pratiyasamutpada** (Sanskrit), **paticcasamuppada** (Pali)
Conditional "coming into being"; "Dependent Origination"

**Samadhi**
Highest level of spiritual meditation

**Samsara** (Sanskrit), **sansara** (Pali)
Cycle of rebirths

**Sangha**
The Buddhist monastic community

**Sanskrit**
The language of the Vedas, language used by Indian scholars

**Shakti**
Female force

**Shakyamuni**
The "Wise one from the family of the Shakya"; the historic Buddha

**Shastra**
Book of teachings, written by philosophers (some of whom are known by name)

**Shatavahana**
Ancient dynasty in Andhra and on the Deccan, supporters of Buddhism

**Shiva**
The Destroyer, Hindu divinity forming, with Brahma and Vishnu, the highest trinity

**Shramana**
Wandering, homeless monk

**Shunyata**
Emptiness, central concept of the Mahayana

**Siddhartha**
First name of the historical Buddha

**Skandha** (Sanskrit), **kandha** (Pali)
The five elements of existence: physical form (*rupa*), feelings (*vedana*), perception (*sanna*), mental processes (*sankhara*), and consciousness (*vinnana*)

**Stupa**
"Topknot," "hill," grave site or monument in the form of a mound or hill

**Sutra**
Text, theme; allegedly the Buddha's original words; in Brahmanism, instructions, explanations of sacrificial rites, etc.

**Tantra**
"Continuum, thread," the basis of Vajrayana Buddhism; also a book or text, instruction in secret teachings

**Tantrism**
Religious teachings founded on the *Tantras*

**Tara**
Goddess in the Mahayana

**Tathagata**
The "One who has gone thus," self-description

of the Buddha (in the Mahayana, essential Buddha nature within each being)

**Thangka**
A painted scroll

**Theravada**
"School of the Elders," a Hinayana sect

**Tipitaka**
See *Pali Canon*

**Triratna**
The "Three Jewels" of Buddhism: the Buddha, the teachings (*dharma*), the monastic community (*sangha*)

**Vairocana**
A *jina*

**Vajra**
Thunderbolt, a diamond scepter

**Vajrayana**
"Diamond Vehicle," the most common form of Tantric Buddhism in Tibet

**Veda**
"Knowledge," holy writings of the Aryan teachings of Vedism, including hymns, magical spells, and sacrificial rites

**Vihara**
Monastery

**Vijnanavada**
See *Cittamatra*

**Vishnu**
The Preserver, Hindu divinity, together with Brahma and Shiva forms the highest trinity

**Yabyum**
Pictorial image of the union of the male (*yab*) and female (*yum*) forces

**Yaksha**
Fertility deity

**Yogacara**
See *Cittamatra*

# Bibliography

## Bibliography

### Introductions and General Works

**Bechert, H., and R. Gombrich,** eds. *The World of Buddhism*. London: Thames and Hudson, 1984.

**Bercholz, Samuel, and Sherab Chödzin Kohn.** *Entering the Stream: An Introduction to the Buddha and His Teachings*. Boston: Shambhala Press, 1993.

**Fischer-Schreiber, Ingrid, Franz-Karl Ehrhard, and Michael S. Diener.** *The Shambhala Dictionary of Buddhism and Zen.* Boston: Shambhala Press, 1991.

**Harvey, Peter.** *An Introduction to Buddhism: Teachings, History and Practices.* Cambridge: Cambridge University Press, 1990.

**Humphreys, Christmas.** *A Popular Dictionary of Buddhism.* Chicago: NTC Publishing, 1997.

**Powell, Andrew.** *Living Buddhism.* London: British Museum Publications, 1989.

**Rhys Davids, T. W.** *Buddhism, Being a Sketch of the Life and the Teachings of Gautama the Buddha.* London: Society for Promoting Christian Knowledge, 1877.

**Snelling, John.** *The Buddhist Handbook: A Complete Guide to Buddhist Teaching and Practice.* London: Century, 1987.

**Yoshinori, Takeuchi, ed.** *Buddhist Spirituality: Indian, Southeast Asian, Tibetan, Early Chinese.* New York: Crossroad, 1995.

### The Historical Buddha

**Chödzin Kohn, Sherab.** *The Awakened One: A Life of the Buddha.* Boston: Shambhala Press, 1994.

**Kulke, Hermann, and Dietmar Rothermund.** *History of India,* 3rd ed. New York: Routledge, 1986.

**Nyanamoli, Bhikku.** *Life of the Buddha.* Kandy, Sri Lanka: Buddhist Publication Society, 1972.

**Pye, M.** *The Buddha.* London: Duckworth, 1979.

**Rhys Davids, T. W.** *Buddhist Birth Stories.* London: Routledge, 1925.

### The Early Teachings

**Conze, Edward, ed. and trans.** *Buddhist Scriptures.* London: Penguin, 1959.

**Jayatilleke, K. N.** *The Message of the Buddha.* New York: Free Press, 1975.

**Harvey, Peter.** *The Selfless Mind–Personality, Consciousness and Nirvana in Early Buddhism.* London: Curzon Press, 1995.

**Rahula, Walpola.** *What the Buddha Taught,* 2nd ed. New York: Grove Press, 1974.

### Hinayana

**Gombrich, R.** *Theravada Buddhism. A Social History from Ancient Benares to Modern Colombo.* London: Routledge and Kegan Paul, 1988

**Mizuno, K.** *The Beginnings of Buddhism,* 3rd ed. Tokyo: Kosei Publishing, 1982.

### Mahayana

**Fatone, V.** *The Philosophy of Nagarjuna.* Delhi: Motilal Banarsidass, 1981.

**Hanh, Thich Nhat.** *Being Peace.* Berkeley: Parallax Press, 1987.

**Lindtner, C.** *Nagarjuniana: Studies in the Writings and Philosophy of Nagarjuna.* Copenhagen: Akademisk forlag, 1982.

**Shantideva, A.** *A Guide to the Bodhisattva's Way of Life,* trans. Stephen Batchelor and Sherpa Tulku. Dharamsala: Library for Tibetan Works and Archives, 1979.

**Suzuki, D. T.** *On Indian Mahayana Buddhism.* New York: Harper, 1968.

**Thurman, Robert A. F.,** trans. *The Holy Teaching of Vimalakirti: A Mahayana Scripture.* University Park: Pennsylvania State University Press, 1974.

**Williams, P.** *Mahayana Buddhism.* New York: Routledge, 1989.

### Tantrayana

**Dasgupta, S. B.** *An Introduction to Tantric Buddhism.* Berkeley: Shambhala, 1974.

**Tsogyal, Yeshe.** *The Lotus Born: The Life Story of Padmasambhava,* trans. Erik Pema Kunsang. Boston: Shambhala, 1993.

**Wayman, A.** *Introduction to the Buddhist Tantric Systems.* Delhi: Motilal Banarsidass, 1981.

### Tibetan Buddhism

**Blofeld, J.** *The Tantric Mysticism of Tibet: A Practical Guide.* Boston: Shambhala, 1987.

# Bibliography

Snellgrove, D. L. *Indo-Tibetan Buddhism: Indian Buddhists and Their Tibetan Successors.* London: Serindia Publications, 1987.

## Buddhism in East Asia

Chen, K. *Buddhism in China.* Princeton: Princeton University Press, 1964.

Franck, Frederick, ed. *The Buddha Eye: An Anthology of the Kyoto School.* New York: Crossroad, 1991.

Suzuki, Shunryu. *Zen Mind, Beginner's Mind: Informal Talks on Zen Meditation and Practice.* New York: Weatherhill, 1970.

Wright, Arthur F. *Buddhism in Chinese History.* Stanford: Stanford University Press, 1959, rpt. 1971.

## Buddhist Art and Architecture

Bhattacharya, B. *The Indian Buddhist Iconography.* Calcutta: Firma K. L. Mukhopadhyay, 1968.

Fisher, Robert E. *Buddhist Art and Architecture.* London: Thames and Hudson, 1993.

Harle, J. C. *The Art and Architecture of the Indian Subcontinent.* London: Penguin, 1986.

Huntington, Susan L. *The Art of Ancient India: Buddhist, Hindu, Jain.* New York: Weather Hill, 1985.

Snellgrove, D. L., ed. *The Image of the Buddha.* New York: Kodansha International, l978.

Sullivan, Michael. *The Arts of China,* 3d ed. Berkeley: University of California Press, 1984.

Tucci, G. *Tibetan Painted Scrolls.* Rome: Libreria dello Stato, 1949, rpt. Kyoto: 1980.

Yanagi, Soetsu. *The Unknown Craftsman: A Japanese Insight into Beauty.* New York: Kodansha International, 1972.

## Buddhism in the West

Dumoulin, H., and Maraldo, J. C., eds. *Buddhism in the Modern World.* New York: Macmillan, 1966.

Prebish, C. S. *American Buddhism.* North Scituate, MA: Duxbury Press, 1979.

Tulku, Tarthang. *Reflections of Mind: Western Psychology Meets Tibetan Buddhism.* Emeryville, CA: Dharma, 1975.

## Online information:

Keown, D., and C. S. Prebish, *Journal of Buddhist Ethics.*
http://www.psu.edu/jbe/jbe.html
and
http://www.gold.ac.uk/jbe/jbe.html

# List of Important Buddhist Shrines

## List of Important Buddhist Shrines

**Afghanistan:**
Cave monasteries with colossal statues of the Buddha in Bamiyan (c. 3rd/4th–7th c.)

**Bangladesh:**
Ruins of Paharpur (8th–12th c.) and Mainamati (7th–13th c.)

**Burma (Myanmar):**
Stupas, temples, and monasteries of the Shrikshetra (5th–9th c.), Pagan (10th–13th c.), and Pegu (from 14th c.), wooden architecture of Mandalay (18th and 19th c.), Shwedagon Pagoda in Rangoon (from 14th c. on)

**China:**
Caves of Yun-kang (5th–8th c.) and Lung-men (6th–9th c.), reliefs and monastery Lingyin Si in Hangzhou (4th–12th c.), caves with murals in Dunhuang, Bezeklik, Turfan, Khocho, Kizil, and Miran (4th–13th c.), temple of Wutai Shan (1st–15th c.), and Emei Shan (2nd–19th c.), colossal statue of Leshan (719–803), Dayan and Xiaoyan Ta in Xian (7th c.), Baita Si in Bejing (11th c.), Famen Si (2nd–9th c.), Chan monastery Shaolin near Lo-yang (5th/6th c.–present), and Chan Temple of Chengdu (6th–17th c.)

**India:**
Monuments of Sanchi (2nd c. BC–6th c. AD), ruins of Sarnath (3rd/2nd c. BC–12th c. AD), Bodh Gaya (from the Mauryan era—Mahabodhi Temple 2nd–14th c.), cave temples on the Deccan, especially Bhaja (1st c. BC), Karla (2nd c. AD), Ajanta (with murals, 2d BC–8th c. AD) and Ellora (5th–7th c., later caves there are Hindu), monastery of Nalanda (5th–12th c.)

**Indonesia:**
Borobudur, Tjandi Mendut, Tjandi Kalasan, Tjandi Plaosan, and Tjandi Sewu, all near Yogyakarta/Java (9th c.), Tjandi Jago near Malang/Java (13th c.)

**Japan:**
Horyuji and Hokkiji (7th c.), Toshodaiji and Shin-Yakushiji (8th c.), all of which are in or near Nara, Byodoin (11th c.) in Uji, Ishiyamadera (12th c.) near Otsu, Great Buddha (1252) in the Engakuji of Kamakura (Zen Center), Daitokuji (starting in the 15th c.) and Ninnaji (17th c.) in Kyoto

**Cambodia:**
Bayon in Angkor (12th/13th c.)

**Korea:**
Pulguk-sa Temple and Sokkur-am Cave in Kyongju (8th c.)

**Laos:**
That Luong and Vat Ho Pra Keo in Vientiane (16th c.), monuments in Luang Prabang (15th–19th c.)

**Nepal:**
Stupas Svayambhunath (from 5th c.), Bodhnath (5th c.) and Chabahil (from ca. 3d c. BC), monuments of Lumbini and Patan (both starting 3rd c. BC)

**Pakistan:**
Ruins around Taxila and Mardan (center of Gandhara), as well as in the Swat Valley (ca. 3rd c. BC–7th c. AD)

**Sri Lanka:**
Ruins of Anuradhapura and Mihintale (3rd c. BC–10th c. AD), also Polonnaruwa (8th–13th c.), colossal Buddha statue of Aukana (ca. 5th c.), Dalada Maligawa (Temple of the Tooth) in Kandy (from the 18th c., a spiritual center, but unimportant in art history)

**Thailand:**
Wat Haripunchai (9th–15th c.) and Wat Kukut (12th/13th c.) in Lamphun, ruins of Ayuthya and Wat Mahathat in Phitsanulok (14th–18th c.), Cedis of Sukhothai (13th–15th c.), edifices of Lopburi (10th–17th c.) and Kampheng Phet (14th–16th c.), monasteries in Thonburi and Bangkok (18th/19th c.)

**Tibet:**
Jokhang in Lhasa (from 7th/8th c.), monasteries of Samye (from 8th c.) and Drepung (15th c.), Kumbum Chorten in Gyantse (15th c.)

**Uzbekistan:**
Monasteries of the Kushan era near Termes and in the valley of Surkandarya

**Vietnam:**
Stupa of Binh Son (11th/12th c.), caves of Ben Duc (from 16th c.), Chua But Thap in Dinh To (from 13th c.), Chua Tay Phuong in Thach Xa (from 8th c.)

# Index of Names

# Index of Names

Olcott, Henry Steel,
American occultist 179
Oldenberg, Hermann,
German translator 179

**P**admasambhava, Indian
scholar 108–109, 113
Perls, Fritz S., co-founder of
Gestalt therapy 181
Phagpa, Tibetan grand lama
115
Poros, Indian king 48
Prasenajit, king of Koshala
20

**R**ahula, son of the Buddha
24
Rhys Davids, Thomas Wil-
liams, British translator
179
Rinchen Zangpo, Tibetan
scholar 110
Ryotan, Japanese Zen
master 148

**S**akya Pandita, Tibetan
grand lama 115
Schopenhauer, Arthur,
German philosopher 178
Schrödinger, Erwin,
physicist 183
Sengai, Japanese Zen
master 145, 146

Shakyamuni, See *Buddha,
historical*
Shariputra, disciple of the
Buddha 24, 50, 52
Shashanka, Benghal king
17
Shenrab Miro, Tibetan
scholar 107
Shinran Shonin, Japanese
reformer 142
Shotoku, Japanese prince
140
Shuddhodana, father of the
Buddha 12, 13, 14, 15
Siddharta Gautama see
Buddha, historical
Sihanuk, Cambodian prince
63–65
Sönam Gyatso, 1st Dalai
Lama 116
Songtsen Gampo, Tibetan
king 106
Suzuki, Daisetz Teitaro,
scholar of Japanese Zen
181

**T**ilopa, Tibetan sorcerer
114
Tokusan, Japanese Zen
master 148
Trapusa, disciple of the
Buddha 18, 22
Tri Rapaltshen 106

Trisong Detsen, Tibetan
scholar 106
Tsongkhapa, Tibetan
reformer 115
Turner, Tina, singer 145

**U**dayana, Indian king
162–163
Udraka Ramaputra,
Brahman scholar 16

**V**aspa, friend of the Buddha
22
Vasubandhu, co-founder of
yogacara 80, 107

**X**uan-zang, Chinese pilgrim
69, 79, 129, 132, 136,
162

**Y**ajnavalkya, Brahman
scholar 20
Yasha, disciple of the
Buddha 22
Yeshesod, Tibetan king
110
Yosodhara, wife of the
Buddha 15

# Picture Credits